The Last Prime Minister

The Last Prime Minister

Being Honest About the UK Presidency

Graham Allen MP

ia

IMPRINT ACADEMIC

Published in the UK by Imprint Academic
PO Box 200, Thorverton EX5 5YX, UK

Published in the USA by Imprint Academic
Philosophy Documentation Center
PO Box 7147, Charlottesville, VA 22906-7147, USA

ISBN 0 907845 41X

A CIP catalogue record for this book is available from the
British Library and US Library of Congress

Contents

To Allyson and Grace
who daily teach me about leadership

Foreword

"The Prime Minister's role as head of Her Majesty's Government, her principal adviser and as Chairman of the Cabinet are not defined in legislation. These roles, including the exercise of power under the Royal Prerogative, have evolved over many years, drawing on convention and usage, and it is not possible precisely to define them. The Government has no plans to introduce legislation in this area."

Tony Blair
15 October 2001
Parliamentary answer to the author

Acknowledgements

I would like to place on record my thanks to those who inspired this essay. John Smith, Labour Party leader 1992–4 who showed that leadership of the Labour Party must combine the visionary with the practical. Tony Blair, for leading my party to the first Labour government for 18 years and then giving me the opportunity to serve in it. He generously scheduled two interviews neither of which could take place in the immediate aftermath of the terrible events of September 11, 2001. My wife Allyson and Professor Michael Genovese who encouraged me to put these thoughts into words. Richard Heller who proofed the draft. The House of Commons Library staff who answered lots of questions. Shirley Stephenson who turned scrawl and scribble into a lovely typescript. Professor Peter Hennessy, Professor Anthony King, Edward Pearce, Wilf Stevenson and many serving ministers and officials of No 10 who would rather not be named, for their advice and conversation over the years.

Preface to Second Edition

The member for Nottingham North rose to his feet, the House of Commons, packed as usual for Prime Ministers Questions, fell silent. "Would the Prime Minister tell this House of Commons by what right, what authority does he — unelected as his office is, by Parliament or the people – believe he can take our country to war and much else, without the formal involvement of Parliament or the people? How can he lecture others about the rule of law when his own legitimacy is so tenuous?" The PM reddened and spluttered replying "Golly y'know I've never even thought about it like that, but you are right. I'll get straight on it and sort out this constitutional nonsense so all of us, the electorate included, can understand our political system and the position of my Office in it".

In your dreams Graham!

But there is, as always, a serious point, for as I wrote these lines, thousands of British soldiers were being sent overseas to prepare for a conflict and to execute the international policy of our government and its major ally. The decision to send them, and the policy which prompted it, were made and chosen by the Prime Minister: he did not require, nor did he seek, the approval of Parliament. The process of "target drift" by the American administration, by which Iraq rather than Al-Qu'aida became the prime enemy, was accepted by the Prime Minister without reference to Parliament, and possibly without formal reference to the cabinet. The actual use of our forces in combat, our military and international strategy during and after the conflict, the terms of any ceasefire or lasting settlement: these too are decisions for the Prime Minister, and he can take them without needing to consult Parliament or even meeting it.

To all intents and purposes, a Prime Minister has the same power over our forces as Henry V, although without the same obligation to lead them in person. Nearly six centuries after Agincourt, Parliament still has no formal or agreed role in the decision to go to war or the conduct and purpose of a war. Parliament does not even have access to the legal advice which would enable it to determine whether a war, or a particular military operation, would be lawful.

The role — or non-role — of Parliament in a conflict against Iraq is the most dramatic demonstration of my primary thesis in the first edition of *The Last Prime Minister*, just over a year ago. The UK Prime Ministership is in effect an unelected, unacknowledged Presidency, and because it is unacknowledged it has none of the checks and balances which normally go with a Presidency. The contrast between the British Parliament and the US Congress over Iraq could not be starker: one a creature of the executive and a spectator of policy and decision-making, the other with powers, duties, advice and a mandate independent of the executive, and an active partner in the conduct of policy.

Yet, at the very moment when the country can see how little its elected MPs can influence the most crucial decision to be made by its government, the Prime Minister resists the inclusion of any elected members of a reformed upper house — for fear that it would challenge "the supremacy of the House of Commons". Ministers manage to use this phrase without a smile on their faces, but in doing so they confirmed my secondary thesis in *The Last Prime Minister* — the British people will never come to grips with the realities of Prime Ministerial power until they and MPs in Parliament strip away the comforting myths which surround the unwritten British constitution. The supremacy of the House of Commons... parliamentary sovereignty ... democratic accountability are myths of this kind, and so long as people believe them, they allow the executive to maintain its apparatus of power without anyone noticing.

The past year therefore confirmed my theses about the true nature of Prime Ministerial power and the role of constitutional myths in sustaining it. However, it did not vindicate my optimism that it would be recognized and reformed. I had hoped that as the costs of excessive Prime Ministerial power became more apparent — not least to the present incumbent — there would be more willingness to share its burdens with other democratic institutions, both national and local. I had hoped that Tony Blair would confirm his place in history by becoming the first Prime Minister to describe accurately the nature of his office and to relax its monopoly powers both to initiate policy and to manage public services even to the micro level.

So far I have been wrong. The UK Presidency remains unchecked, and it has shown no willingness to seek partnership with the legislature, or the wider nation, even when such a partnership would clearly assist its objectives. Over Iraq, the Prime Minister could have reinforced his influence over American policy if he had sought the support of Parliament. He chose not to do so, and his efforts to persuade the US administration to use the United Nations and to build a coalition against Iraq relied only on a punishing programme of personal diplomacy. Similarly, the Prime Minister's drive to reform the policies and institutions of the EU would have benefited from an active partnership with Parliament and indeed with British public opinion in general. Instead, it relied on the traditional methods of personal deal-making behind closed doors. On these issues, and many others, not least terrorism, the UK legislature shares the fundamental objectives of the UK Presidency and wants to help achieve them: its continued impotence and irrelevance are a loss to good government and public involvement.

Nevertheless, democratic reformers must cling to the hope of breakthrough and to faith in the triumph of a just cause, regardless of the objective situation. The past year has brought signs that the UK Presidency is becoming a little more flexible, and the UK legislature a little less supine.

For example, the current Prime Minister has generously agreed to appear before Parliament's Liaison Committee (the chairs of all Commons committees) twice a year, although the reader will have to judge whether the chairs can make this more than an extension to the Presidential press conferences, announced at the same time.[1]

At a more mundane level, the executive has allowed Parliament to give itself a more sensible calendar and hours of work, to make select committees more effective, and to conduct pre-legislative scrutiny of bills. However, the daily and long- term parliamentary agenda and the appointment of select committee chairs remain in the control of the Prime Minister. Although two popular MPs were saved against the government's wishes by a surprise backbench rebellion, it is still generally true to say that committee chairs hold their office on sufferance from the government. Nor have they been given the salary, status and independent career structure recommended by the Modernization Committee.

Pre-legislative scrutiny likewise depends on the goodwill of the executive, and few departmental ministers have so far been willing to take the extra time to publish bills in draft. For example the government's flagship Criminal Justice Bill for session 2002-03 has 273 densely-packed clauses and 26 schedules with major implications for the public's experience of crime and the criminal justice system. It was an ideal candidate for extended pre-legislative scrutiny: it did not receive it, and it will therefore not benefit from the detailed comments of either professional experts or the victims of crime which it is meant to serve. Such scrutiny on-line will one day allow all electors to improve the laws which govern them.

---

[1]   The latter is an interesting example of the ambiguous effects of self-reform by the Presidency. On the face of it, the new-style conference widens the Prime Minister's accountability: instead of being questioned by the narrow circle of Lobby correspondents he faces a much broader range of journalists from many different media organizations. But critics suggest that the widening will produce softer, less penetrating questions — thus weakening accountability. Again the reader will have to judge.

Although these weaknesses remain, the year has shown the executive willing to contemplate, and even promote, house-keeping improvements for the work of the legislature. More important, it has shown the legislature fighting back against the extremes of executive power.

On Iraq, the executive was actually forced to recall Parliament ahead of time. I was fortunate to co-ordinate MPs from all parties who showed that they were prepared to meet and debate the crisis on their own initiative. The first independent Parliament since 1640 was only five days from meeting, before the government gave way. At the time of writing, about half the backbench MPs of all parties have endorsed proposals to allow the Speaker, as well as the government, to recall Parliament in a future crisis and to give the UK Parliament, like the US Congress, the right to be consulted about war. However, party partisanship has so far prevented a united parliamentary vote against the executive on these issues.

On second chamber reform, while the Prime Minister's preference for a wholly appointed chamber has been defeated, his decision to allow a plethora of options and votes left no alternative with a majority. It also further humiliated a House of Commons that was seen to be incapable of independent thought and unable to rise above personal and party backbiting to seize the opportunity of once-in-a-generation reform. The executive remained strong and unchallenged and Parliament was left less relevant and in even greater contempt — the perfect outcome for the Presidency.

It is conceivable that the House, rather than the government, will write its own bill on Lords reform, as it will do with foxhunting. But laughably neither can progress in the legislature without the executive's consent.

However, the creation of a balanced democratic constitution for our country will not be achieved by cautious piecemeal concessions by the executive nor by fitful revolts from the legislature. If the two sides cannot admit the nature of the problem of unacknowledged Presidential power, it will be impossible for them to work out a solution.

In the first edition I stressed that a dose of honesty and self-awareness was the pre-requisite for action. Tony Blair supplied some of these at the Liaison Committee on 16 July 2002 when he said:

> I am openly avowing that [sc. his belief in a strong executive Premiership]. I am saying that this is the right thing to do...I cannot believe there is a single Prime Minister...who has not wanted the Prime Minister's writ to run. I cannot believe there is a Prime Minister sitting in Downing Street saying, "Let them just get on with it". It is not the real world. The real world is that with the Prime Minister the buck stops with you; that is the top job and that is how it should be.

This is as close as any Prime Minister has ever come to "coming out" as President.

Tony Blair also told the Liaison Committee on 16 July that: "One thing I do say...very strongly is that I make no apology for having a strong centre." He gave two reasons for this. Firstly, there was "the focus of this Government...on delivering better public services" to which he argued "it is...absolutely vital for the centre to play a role." Secondly, international security issues meant that "a lot more...needs to be done at Prime Ministerial level."

Equally the span of the UK President's office continues to spread, its functions ever more difficult to conceal. In June 2002, Sir Andrew Turnbull, due to replace Sir Richard Wilson as Cabinet Secretary, set out his plans for the next three years. When describing what he saw as the "four main roles" of the Cabinet Office, the first item on Turnbull's list was "to support the Prime Minister in leading the Government." Turnbull also referred to a number of units, located in the Cabinet Office, which were effectively answerable to the Prime Minister. For example, the Strategy Unit would work confidentially "to the Prime Minister" and support Lord Birt, the Prime Minister's Strategy Adviser, while the Delivery Unit would "report regularly to the PM through the Minister for the Cabinet Office." The Presidential Department is all but an officially acknowledged fact.

A pessimistic analyst would see an unimaginative and homogenous government entering its sixth year, a muscle-bound centre with a brain but without the certainty and sense of purpose in government which its late leader John Smith possessed. We see a President compelled not only to supply an ideology and a value-system for his government but also to play a hands-on role in almost every area of government (although virtually excluded by his Chancellor from the area which matters most), while simultaneously meeting the insatiable demands of the modern media. He would note the loss to the President of two key confidants, Peter Mandelson and Anji Hunter, while the two other key Presidential advisors, Alastair Campbell and Jonathan Powell, both need sabbaticals to recharge and regroup.

This President, and his circle, need some relief from the incessant responsibility of making our government work. However an unelected, unacknowledged Presidency allows no respite, no partners, no powersharing, no joint responsibility, and no admissions of fallibility to a voracious press. Exhaustion, defeat, humiliation are the only possible endings to a political career in a unitary system. Any attempt to create a more sensible, humane and effective form of government will first have to confront and refute the charge of weakness or evasion from the only remaining institution which the Presidency fears — the media.

The pessimist might conclude that Labour must be defeated, and spend an indeterminate time in opposition, before it thinks through its next contribution to Britain's democracy. That prospect is unpalatable — even unthinkable. The restoration of a Tory government, and the wilful destruction of all of Labour's achievements in rebuilding public services and creating opportunity for all in society, would be a terrible price to pay to refresh our vision.

Fortunately it is still possible to be an optimist. Hope springs eternal that the case for democracy is so strong as to convince a bright intelligent leadership — this one or the next — to adopt it as the central guiding principle of government. Such a leadership would use democratic renewal to arrest the continuing decline in party enthusiasm and membership, regenerate public interest and participation and turn a coasting administration into a moral crusade.

I am painfully aware that Richard Crossman expressed a similar optimism forty years ago in the introduction to his edition of
Bagehot's *The English Constitution*:

> In theory — but also in practice — the British people retains the
> power not merely to choose between two Prime Ministers, and two
> parties, but to throw off its deferential attitude and reshape the
> political system, making the parties instruments of popular control,
> and even insisting that the House of Commons should once again
> provide the popular check on the executive. It is my hope and belief
> that this will happen.

Since Crossman expressed this "hope and belief" (in 1963)
almost all the movement has been in the wrong direction,
towards an over-mighty executive with an enfeebled Parliament
and an apathetic, disaffected democracy. As a result, there is a
serious danger that the focus of political activity will move
beyond Parliament and elected representative institutions.
Modern history shows how dangerous this is. The failure of
Crossman's hopes makes it all the more urgent now to recognize
what Britain's government has become. Unless we acknowledge
honestly the UK Presidency and check and balance its powers
and responsibilities we will not only condemn present and
future occupants to exhaustion but delay the possibility of
democracy and good government for our country. The incumbent's responsibility is not to the Prime Ministership but to the
nation and our democracy.

The great qualities of the current Prime Minister are still not
properly appreciated by the party which he has restored to
greatness. However the quality of vision which made Labour
electable must now be re-applied to give Labour, indeed democratic politics, a future. "We are at our best when we are at our
boldest", as Tony Blair rightly reminded his party. The time for
the leadership's next move is approaching — either boldly forward into a modern constitution or boldly aside, to pass the
torch of democratic reform to a successor.

House of Commons
February 2003

Introduction

Political power in the UK is concentrated in No. 10 Downing Street and Whitehall. Yet the daily theatre of parliamentary politics makes further political analysis difficult, not least for parliamentarians. When it has to be viewed through the distorting lens of the media — whose interest is to play up the sensational, the trivial and the personal, it becomes ever more awkward for any of us to take serious stock of where Britain's political development has got to and where it is going. This is particularly so when trying to discuss seriously such a politically loaded and heavily caricatured concept as "Presidentialism". *I use the term UK Presidency as a description not an accusation.* Equally I write of the Prime Ministership as a concept and not of individual Prime Ministers unless pertinent.

I will attempt to step back and see the big picture — whenever possible without a partisan eye. Having served in the Labour government for the past four years has, hopefully, helped with some insights. Often those inside government who are most in need of an open discussion on these issues are those most inhibited, not least because they are fearful of the random nature of Prime Ministerial patronage, I am happy here to serve as a proxy for many of them.

I have attempted to write, not for any party advantage, but more in the spirit of an open letter to the current and future Prime Ministers to help light a way forward and in a small way assist the progress of British politics so that electors, and perhaps even some practising politicians, might better understand their democracy, and its potential. The continuing trend towards

lower turnouts in UK elections and deeper political cynicism as
well as external threats to democracy make it ever more important that we understand our own, unique democracy, constantly
maintain it and develop a wish and a will to sustain and develop
it.

Summary

Those who have a limited attention span may wish just to scan
the text for the *italics*. For journalists, MPs and other such bluff-
ers the summary is:
- The UK has, in effect, a Presidency
- We should recognise it
- We should welcome it
- We should democratically control it

Chapter 1

The Origins of the UK Presidency

Ask most British people what a President is and they will bring to mind the image of an all-powerful, central, single figure who dominates the political process. While this is an oversimplification — particularly in nations that have developed clear, written constitutions and democratic practice — it nonetheless helps us make a start in our examination of the British Presidency.

Equally, the office of Prime Minister is often seen through British eyes as being the first among equals, a key representative of a collegiate system of government. In other words while this minister may be prime, he or she is but the centre of a web of connections and constraints linking a swathe of elected colleagues. My first contention — not an original one — is that *the Prime Ministerial model is no longer the best way of understanding the way in which Britain is governed.*

I make no simple analogy that we in the UK have an American system of government or that we could, or should, transplant the US Presidency into very different British soil. The form of the UK Presidency is as unique as the UK's own politics and history. It is a far from complete or perfect definition but as a concept and a tool will become ever more valuable in understanding British politics. I use the term UK Presidency as the best summary of a trend and to reveal a truth about UK politics.

Even the idea of defining a Presidency and a Prime Ministership is fraught with difficulty. Most contemporary examples of the Presidency, notably in the US, rest upon well-defined constitutional rules and judicially tested precedents. This cannot be said of the Prime Ministership, which is an evolving concoction, unlimited by written rules and regulations and shrouded in mystery. One example of the latter is that after nearly 300 years of Prime Ministers, *UK law makes no comprehensive reference to the office of Prime Minister* — those statutory references that do exist relate largely to appointments. This government has proved that obstacles to statutory definition are easily overcome since they have legally defined the roles of the first ministers of Scotland, Wales and Northern Ireland.

Although no set of founding fathers consciously sat down and agreed we were to have a UK Presidency, I hope to make it evident that *unplanned and imperfect as it is, we are for all intents and purposes ruled by a hidden Presidency*. It is not that such a high profile office is a secret, more that it would be impolite to talk about it openly. For the British it may be the very fact that it has never been publicly and explicitly proclaimed that makes it difficult for us to accept the current reality — it may be real but it is not "official". Part of what I am trying to achieve here is to help us all *honestly confront the truth of the UK Presidency, thereby being better able to deal with it. Getting the current Prime Minster to "come out" as President will be a key moment.*

The Failed Revolution

The concept of a UK Presidency — one which is not directly legitimised by the electorate — also helps us understand the massive imbalances that have developed between the various parts of an unwritten constitution. *Presidential power in the US is compromised, in the UK it is not.* There is no careful weighing and weighting of institutional power here, no jealously guarded checks and balances. In other words there is no conscious separation of powers. Instead of healthy balance we have an executive (the UK Presidency) which stands like an 800 lb gorilla alongside a wizened legislature and judiciary. They stand like cowed and malnourished dependants, the latest victims of generations of abuse accepted as normality, rather than separate, lively checks on the executive.

One of the key pillars of Western democracy is the concept of the separation of powers — the healthy interaction and controlled competition of executive, legislature and judiciary first elaborated by Montesqieu in 1748. This was taken into political practice by the US founding fathers who built into their system a clear definition of the respective powers of the institutions and a deliberate system of checks and balances. These fundamentals have subsequently been adopted by, or aspired to, by most democracies. Recent democratic changes pioneered by the Labour government represent the first step in this direction and serious break with the UK's constitutional tradition of muddle, evolution and secrecy.

If the UK does not now take this further and seek to devise a rational, conscious system of government then we will have achieved little more than mitigating the worst excesses of the "divine right" to rule. In many ways the fact that the first western democratic revolution took place in England in the 1640s is responsible for much of our subsequent path. It was the pioneer, but it took place decades before the maturation of the political thought that could have sustained it. Hence it was partial and ill formed, unable ultimately to survive. While progress was undoubtedly made, the restoration of the monarchy and the deal between it and the elite represented in Parliament in 1688 repositioned the ruling classes so that they were effectively inoculated against further radical change of the sort which later swept Western nations. Thereafter the UK was largely bypassed by the key democratic debates of the time, symbolised by Thomas Paine's works — which sparked and inspired revolutions in France and America, but led only to prison terms for his British publishers.

In the sweep of history this meant the UK was largely unhindered in evolving towards a unitary state power where the executive and legislature were fused rather than separated. To use a modern analogy, in US terms this is the equivalent of one person being the President as well as the majority leader in Congress (and then some).When President Clinton spoke to the British cabinet in Downing Street after Labour's 1997 electoral landslide he remarked enviously on the new Prime Minister's control, not only of the executive but of the legislature — something he constitutionally could never have.[1] The UK Presidency has some very large knobs on indeed. Yet in the UK accident rather than conscious design is the hallmark of our unwritten constitution. In order to understand the enigma of our unwritten constitution, and indeed British politics in general, one has to crack the code of executive power.

It has always been harder to see the division of powers in the tangled British state than in other countries. We have never put our executive, our legislature and our judiciary into neat separate packages. The monarch not only exercised executive power but also made law and dispensed justice. (Even today, the Queen is still the fount of justice and she can still create law directly by Orders in Council.) Our Parliament is not only a law maker and a seat of government but a court of justice: our highest justices, the law lords, are ex officio members of one house of Parliament. Our judges and magistrates have not only interpreted the law but created it, and by long tradition and practice they exercise many acts of executive power (including such curiosities as issuing licenses to public houses).

Unlike the American founding fathers, British politicians and thinkers, such as John Locke, grew out of the premature English Revolution and did not value the separation of power so much as the balance of power. They sought a political system which would steer the nation (and particularly its property owners) between the two extremes of anarchy and tyranny. The search for this balance pre-occupied most seventeenth-century thinkers and politicians. It ended with the creation of an elective monarchy chosen by Parliament. William III became king through Parliament. Every single one of Queen Anne's successors has been sovereign through an act of Parliament (the Act of Settlement 1701) not in hereditary right. Parliament's success led to a

---

[1] "I would love to have a 179 seat majority", *Financial Times*, 30 May 1997.

new organ of executive power — the premiership. The holder of this office had to be a member of either house of Parliament; his power derived from Parliament and could be terminated by Parliament.

First Among Equals

The first holder of this as yet unacknowledged office — Sir Horace Walpole — was also the first MP to be the chief minister of the British government. The length of his term of his office 1721–42 (which no one has yet beaten) derived not from his sovereign's choice, still less the will of the people, or the power of the media — but from his mastery of the eighteenth century House of Commons. Walpole spent long hours in the House and developed an acute, detailed knowledge of all its members, thereby inaugurating a long golden age of parliamentary power.

From Walpole to the mid-nineteenth century the British political system managed to balance a successful premiership and a successful Parliament. This golden age depended on four factors:

- the absence of democracy, and in consequence, the absence of mass party politics. MPs did not need a party label or a party machine to get themselves elected: many actually owned their constituencies

- the House of Lords had almost equal power and influence to the Commons. Although the Prime Minister could and did hand out peerages to his own placemen, no Prime Minister had control of the full membership of the House of Lords

- there were no mass media. Politicians did not have the need or the means to make themselves known to the wider electorate. At the same time, opinion research was unknown and unnecessary; and

- the functions of the British government were very small by today's standards. Many modern departments of state (Education, Health, Social Security) did not exist at a central level; others had very limited functions (the Treasury simply raised taxes, Trade and Industry enforced weights and measures legislation).

From 1832 onwards, all of these special factors gradually disappeared. The Reform Acts of the nineteenth century enfranchised millions of new voters (joined by women in 1918 and 1928). The mass electorate created a need for mass parties and these parties became virtually the sole means of entry into the House of Commons. (They also became more and more important as a means of entry into the House of Lords, as hereditary peerages died out and were not replaced). Unlike American political parties, whose leadership is temporary and lasts only for Presidential election years, Britain's political parties have a leader permanently in being. With rare exceptions, the party leaders have had firm control over their parties — and because of this they have controlled Parliament.

The House of Lords lost power and status with the Parliament Act of 1911. Far from being able to challenge the Prime Minister it became a new source of Prime Ministerial or party patronage, especially after 1958 when life peerages were introduced. When in 1999 most of the hereditary peers were removed, the Lords became almost entirely an appointed House. Almost every member (even the bishops) owed his or her place to a past or present Prime Minister or party leader.

The advent of mass media in the nineteenth century gave party leaders more opportunity to make themselves known to the British people and to do so independently of Parliament. The media have therefore given party leaders a new source of power at Parliament's expense. A determined and efficient Prime Minister can not only develop his own relationship with the media but also deny the same access to competitors — including Parliament. Allied to his special relationship with the media, a modern Prime Minister or party leader also enjoys special access to sophisticated opinion research. He or she can shape (or more likely, react to) public opinion far quicker than Parliament.

Finally, from the second half of the nineteenth century onwards, central government has taken on more and more responsibilities, particularly during the two world wars which required the total mobilization of the British state. This has produced a massive rise in executive power, completely unmatched by any corresponding growth in the power of parliamentary scrutiny. Indeed Parliament has systematically abdicated much of its power of delay and scrutiny by allowing ministers to effect more and more changes through regulation, statutory instrument or even administrative fiat, rather than introducing primary legislation.

Political legitimacy became synonymous with directly elected representation and as the franchise got wider *electoral legitimacy was monopolised by the Commons*, who in order to execute their parties' objectives, in turn *ceded their political sovereignty to their leaderships*. The more the MP's electability depended upon the public perception of the Prime Minister, the more exclusive became his power. Thus was completed the vacuous circle which characterises British politics today.

For almost 200 years *the British Prime Ministership evolved and adapted in a way that no other political institution was able to*, or allowed to. An awful democratic dysfunction lay at the heart of British politics. By the early part of the twentieth century this asymmetry was such that the executive, selected from the House of Commons, had become dominant, and was checked by nothing more substantial than its own self-control.

Myth of Parliamentary Sovereignty

Lack of formal restraints plus weak institutional barriers meant that little has stood in the way of the development of a Presidency in the UK.

The UK has a history of resistance to written constitutions and entrenched rights. Since these both limit the executive, it is of little surprise that the executive has felt that public ignorance was bliss and has always been reluctant to discuss these issues seriously.

In the US, even with a written constitution, the personality of particular Presidents has sometimes allowed them to push back the often vague boundaries of Presidential power. But the elastic nature of the constitution has led Congress to bounce back when in its turn, it came to be relatively strong. Equally individuals and institutions could use the Supreme Court and judiciary to seek to rebalance an over-mighty executive or legislature. None

of these things were given freely, they resulted from years —
often decades — of debate before a new balance was found. Then
the process would start again. The idea that a written constitution is rigid and inflexible is a nonsense — it is always in a state of
flux and open to constant interpretation. The interpretation,
however, is based upon an open and agreed text available to all,
rather than the imprecision of an unwritten and largely secret
constitution, which has usually meant little more than the ability
of the executive to rewrite the rules for its own convenience.

For 200 years the imperceptible growth in the powers of the
Prime Minister took place behind the rhetoric of parliamentary
sovereignty. There was never a key point where Parliament felt
the power had passed from Crown to Prime Minister. Parliament and parliamentarians mistakenly associated the strengthening of the Prime Ministerial incubus with the strengthening of
Parliament, proximity to power with the use of power. Parliamentarians in the majority could think of it as "our" government
because of the strong party labels and because party policy or
party ideals were being executed. Being a supporter or even a
cheerleader could be passed off as being a high status member of
the team. Even in recent times the delusion of parliamentary
sovereignty has allowed many MPs to *mistake government power
for parliamentary power.* The occasional electoral oddity where
the parliamentary parties are in rough numerical balance being
constantly prayed in aid as proof that we have a viable and effective parliamentary system.

Prime Ministers have also perpetuated these myths — a nod to
Parliament and the chore of occasional attendance are a small
price to pay for the exercise of power from No 10 and Whitehall.
*Making MPs aware of their real status will be one of the first steps to
their realising a separate legislative identity, distinct from government.*

Over two centuries the growth of the party system in British
politics placed ever more authority in the hands of the party
leader so that he came to lead not only his party in the country
but in the legislature too and was de facto candidate for leader of

the executive. The growing dominance of one figure had a dramatic impact upon the legislature and the electoral process.

In consequence, the 2001 general election more than any other previously was a referendum on two Presidential candidates — with individual MPs' results totting up on election night like so many places in an electoral college. While twentieth century MPs worked ever harder in their constituencies, the paradox was their localness had less and less influence on their electorate. Most MPs of all parties have an infinite capacity to delude themselves about their personal vote and personal popularity. The reality is that most electors do not know the name or party of their MP. By May 2001 59% of electors could not identify their own MP (MORI). Traditionally, electors have voted on the party label but they now increasingly vote on the personality of the leading Prime Ministerial candidates. Legislators evolved into *rubber stamps for executive laws* and now have become mere appendages at their own elections, being grateful for the pre-election photo opportunity with the Presidential candidate every four years. What further humiliation is needed to sting MPs into action?

One of the starkest demonstrations of parliamentary impotence is that, after the general election, Parliament, unlike for example the Bundestag, is not even trusted formally to elect the Prime Minister. He is put in place by a royal summons — it is after all Her Majesty's Government which is being formed, not the newly elected Parliament's government, despite what many MPs believe. Thereafter the total patronage exercised by the Prime Minister over the legislature from which the bulk of the executive is drawn is demonstrated by the crudity of the appointment and firing process. Assessment and merit have never figured much in this process. However almost all the constraints of the last century of needing to represent different strands of opinion, regionality and the interests of powerful personalities have been subdued. The diminution of ideology and focus on one personality have, as will be explained later, increasingly added to an already formidable power of patronage.

Hence the House of Commons has in reality evolved to become the House of Government. Out of 412 MPs currently in the majority party, the Prime Minister appoints 142 as ministers and parliamentary private secretaries. At least as many again aspire to such a role. Then 113 get consolation through appointment to Parliament's departmental select committees personally cleared by the Prime Minister. These factors are hardly conducive to producing an alternative view from Parliament which can serve as a serious basis for negotiation and exchange with the executive. For example, until MPs summon up the courage to directly elect their own select committees, Parliament's view will continue to be seen largely as the view of those approved by the executive. The contrast with US Congressional committees, which the executive does not control, is obvious. Hence through the last century it became increasingly evident that even with a massive parliamentary majority, *the power of Prime Ministerial patronage covers the large bulk of his or her parliamentary party*. Equally the smaller the majority the higher the percentage of the parliamentary party covered by patronage and the greater the pressure "not to let the party (i.e. President) down" in a tighter parliamentary situation.

The legislature's second chamber is no more of a check than the first chamber. We have mentioned the historic decline in power of the House of Lords in the twentieth century. By the beginning of the new century it has become an appointive chamber with the Prime Minister having the unique power of appointing legislators in the UK system. While (the non-party) "cross-bench" Lords are now proposed by an outside commission, the Prime Minister still nominates his own party's appointees.

If the second chamber were to be directly elected it could put its own point of view in the public arena and one not beholden to the executive. It is too simplistic to say this is why the executive have been so reluctant to make a serious reform of the second chamber — since the worst excesses of one party rule have been tackled. However the failure to provide for the election of members to one of the houses of the legislature maintains a handy monopoly on electoral legitimacy at national level for the House of Commons and therefore (even though it is indirect) for the Presidency.

These developments over many centuries, the product not of conspiracy but of events, has led to where we are today — "The Lost World" in the evolution of Western democracy. Viewed in economic terms the British political system can be characterised as a *political monopoly* — all power controlled by one player, the UK Chief Executive. In a market this would lead to massive distortion and the inability and unwillingness to respond to its customers, the ability to rig the terms of trade, dictate to suppliers and exclude competition — all of which are evident today in UK politics. To restore health to the market the economist's answer would probably involve a division of the political monopoly into a plurality of independent competing institutions working to a publicly available set of regulations. While creating the perfect political market may be unattainable we certainly can and must make massive improvements before perfection even threatens.

The historic failure to define and protect a separation of powers in the UK meant that the possibility to weld together the executive and legislature always existed. The lack of formal constraints allied to control of the party machine meant that it was inherent in the British political system for Prime Ministers to become dominant.

Clearly the old concepts of the Prime Ministership (first among equals, collegiate, etc.) no longer apply and a different framework for understanding how Britain is governed needs to be applied. The most obvious framework is that of a Presidency. We will examine the strengthening of the Presidency in the UK by reference to contemporary Prime Ministers from Harold Macmillan onward. We should be clear that this is an historical progression, proving that the powers of the Prime Minister have extended through time though with obvious growth spurts under particular dominant personalities, notably Margaret Thatcher.

The potential has always been there. It has taken more recent developments to realise that potential and to make the British Presidency more obvious.

The result is that we entered the modern era with everything in place to create what was to all intents and purposes a Presidency, the potential for a colossus to tower unchallenged over politics in the UK.

Chapter 2

The Modern UK Presidency

The lack of restraints and the historical factors outlined in Chapter 1 would not in themselves have been enough to promote the Presidency as we see it today in the UK. In addition throughout the twentieth century British politics and history had to produce a cocktail of other factors to fertilise the distinctive, indeed unique, UK Presidency of today. Foremost among these factors have been:

- The centralisation of power in British politics
- The role of the modern media
- The end of cabinet government
- The evolution of political parties
- The ethos of the civil service
- The weakening of ideology/personalisation of politics

The impact of these factors in the past 30 years has made it increasingly more difficult to deny the reality of Presidential power. In 1988 it could be written:

> In fact if not in theory, the Prime Minister is Head of State, Chief Executive and Chief Legislator, and while in office is not circumscribed by any clear or binding constitutional limitations. Against this in the UK is not a single alternative source of secure constitutional power at any level.[1]

---

[1]   *The Scottish Claim of Right.*

The Centralisation of Power in the UK

Of all the democratic countries in the Western world the UK has the most centralised system of political and administrative power. Its exclusive fount and focus is the Prime Ministership — it is the product of a failure to have a proper separation of powers in the UK allied to the command structure which evolved to run the world's first industrial revolution, its largest ever empire and later two world wars. Not for Britain the foreign concepts of states' rights as in the USA or powerful regional *Lander* as in Germany or the departments and mayoralties of France. In the UK our power is unitary — a single track to the door of No 10 Downing Street. Whichever personality resides behind its door, however "unpresidential" they may at first appear to be — perhaps a John Major or an Iain Duncan Smith — they are presented with an *inventory of Prime Ministerial power which is awesome*. More than anything else it is the massive political arsenal with rack upon rack of power, authority and influence that comes with the office that makes it a *de facto UK Presidency*.

Firstly he or she is the leader of their political party and its national organisation which has links to every member and councillor in the UK. Secondly, he is not merely a Member of Parliament but the leader of the parliamentary party and as such has total authority to run the majority party in Parliament when an election is won. Thus the whole legislative agenda is in his gift.

After a successful general election the leader of the largest party metamorphoses into a Prime Minister and personally appoints (without any ratification process) every member of the executive — the government ministers — and can remove them at will. As First Lord of the Treasury he outranks the Chancellor on financial matters and as Minister for the Civil Service he is responsible for supervising the civil service which administers the implementation of policy. He can also nominate members to the unelected second chamber: the current Prime Minister has

appointed 116 Labour Peers since May 1997.[2] To complete the
ravaging of the concept of a separation of powers, the Prime
Minister appoints the Lord Chancellor and law officers who in
turn appoint and control the judiciary.

In addition a whole panoply of so called royal prerogative
powers are reserved to the Prime Minister. This massive unaccountable hinterland of executive power includes the making of
treaties, and the ability to go to war. The legal existence and dissolution of Parliament results from royal prerogative. The civil
service and the BBC are also the creation of the executive in this
way.

Of course in true British style all this power is concealed by
acres of window dressing: privy councils, royal audiences, parliamentary rituals, the facades of ancient buildings and public
school accents. While we in the UK would rather chatter about
the cut and colour of the camouflage, behind it the UK President
has power that would make Stalin blush.

The UK presidential quango has developed — without being
directly elected — in a way which has effectively privatised
political power beyond our publicly owned and representative
institutions. The very obscurity of the legitimacy of these powers
causes ignorance about our politics. Myth, magic and mystery
have no place in a modern democracy. The sooner we systematically define and *catalogue these Prime Ministerial powers under
statute,* the sooner will we be able to define the legitimate powers
that we would want and may need the British Presidency to
exercise.

While of course it is appropriate that many functions can only
take place centrally, the sprawling tendrils of a modern
unchecked unitary state can choke the vitality out of the rest of
our political society.

Although it may be the last thing which UK Prime Ministers
want, the blanket of powers of the *UK Presidency inadvertently
suffocates initiative at every lower level.* Ministers in modern government of all parties who want to do more than fill positions

complain privately about not being allowed to get on with the job as they see it, let alone being creative or bold. Modern government is full of bright capable people, many of whom have been deeply frustrated by the top-down culture which they feel they cannot change or influence.

It is not only ministers who can't innovate for fear of their "shadow" at No 10, the whole raft of locally elected government is denied any constitutional independence and legitimacy of its own and is reduced to a mechanical role as agent of the centre, stifling ideas, enterprise and local political activism into the bargain. Public agencies, the health service and local schools are all subject to micro management, targets and plans from the centre.

This over-centralisation also impacts more and more on electoral behaviour. All elections, including those for Members of Parliament, mean less. If the election which indirectly puts in the President is a foregone conclusion, voters may not be motivated to turn out to vote for ever less influential local reasons and ever less relevant local candidates.

With such over-centralisation the UK Presidency and those who serve it can come to feel that the government interest, the party interest and even the national interest can be subsumed within the Presidential interest. To them, not least because of the massive responsibilities of unitary power, it becomes more difficult to see that other interests, while puny, may have a valid and different viewpoint which is entitled to be respected. This has nothing to do with the personal proclivities of individuals who exercise power, but everything to do with the absence of statutory authority and written rules to set the boundaries which can lead to the irresistible temptation to decide first and consult later.

There is every reason to suspect that we have *not witnessed the end of the growth of Presidential powers in the UK*. In my brief political lifetime, which began with Harold Wilson, the day-to-day accretion of power by the centre over the details of local government, the NHS and education has shown no sign of diminishing. Equally, as new areas of importance open up — for example terrorism, globalisation, the media, new technology — centralised political power has the strength to be first to colonise and monopolise its political use and access.

In the last century people (including Prime Ministers themselves) were less conscious of the power and spread of the UK Presidency because they were in the middle of its evolution. We have no such excuse. The power of the UK Presidency is sprayed on our eyeballs daily. The question now is do we and the UK Presidency itself view this as a problem if left to continue unchecked, and if so, do we have the capacity and the will to do something about it?

The Modern Media

As much as any other factor, it is the emergence of minute–to-minute political coverage which has allowed the Prime Ministership to make the quantum leap to a British Presidency in recent years. It is now the *media not the party who are crucial to securing electoral victory*, they must therefore be kept onside and serviced at all times.

I am never sure if there was a golden age when thoughtful political columnists sucked on their pipes and penned elegant essays on the nature of power — although newspapers used to carry long factual reports on politics, including verbatim texts of major political speeches. What is certain however is that today's media demand one talking head that speaks for the whole of the party and government. Such a service must be virtually on demand and offer well crafted, pre-digested soundbites which minimise the need for effort from journalists and, even more important, from readers and listeners. Thirty or so lobby correspondents have stories to write every day, "Government doing pretty well, not much happening" is not one of them. *If Britain did not have a President the media would need to invent one*, a constant pole star and point of reference and quotations.

The media do not merely report, they impact upon the form taken by the British executive. A British Prime Minister could never again be collegiate even to the limited extent of Jim Callaghan. The media would portray this as weakness, not strength. You have to be a President even if you do not want to be. John Major inherited greater powers and status in the Prime Ministership than any of his predecessors, but it often appeared that he could not or would not use that power and consequently he was damned for this by much of the media.

The media — television and radio in particular — are complicit in building up this unitary one-track politics and undermining pluralism. Every MP has found that it is very hard to get access to television, above all to explain a complicated issue, unless he or she is opposed to (or accept that they will be depicted as being opposed to) the leadership and government. TV and radio cut out the wide debate and promote only the Prime Minister (or a proxy) and an oppositionist. This is bad for the diversity and quality of serious political debate.

It is a tremendous drain on the Prime Minister and his staff in feeding the beast of the media on an almost permanent basis. A holding comment by a Prime Minister who has yet to consult cabinet colleagues is no longer tenable. The comment must be speedy yet carefully thought out — for it can be quoted back days or years later. Anything the media regard as newsworthy means the PM "must take charge" or at least have a fully defensible view. Despite protestations from No 10 about the current PM's focus, I expect 50% of his daily mental energy and that of his office goes on media related matters [see appendix 5].

In the UK Presidency's relationship with the media *it is not what you do so much as how it comes across.* The danger that is dealing with the perception is not always the same as dealing with the substance. Effective presentation and the management of discontent is essential in modern politics but it should lay alongside — and is not to be confused with — democratic accountability. Some UK Presidents are better than others at this media relationship and all complain about it. However none have yet been prepared to change the relationship with the media by accepting limits to their authority, or by developing the responsibilities of other legitimate political institutions. The motto appears to be "better the devil you can spin".

Many have argued that the media have become Her Majesty's Government's Loyal Opposition — so contemptuous of Parliament's feebleness that they have a duty to take it on themselves to make life hard for the Presidency. Be that as it may, it is in the media's interest to maintain their symbiosis with the Presidency. They like this role, with its twice a day access to the heart of power through the No 10 media briefing, and enjoy being courted and flattered — occasionally biting the hand that feeds it, as if to demonstrate independence. It is not in the media's interest to share power even with legitimate institutions like Parliament, let alone to help reformers build alternatives which would make the media's lives more complicated. This is a trait they share with the Presidency.

The mutual pre-occupation of this media/Presidency relationship finds its culmination in the role of the Prime Minister's Press Secretary as its ringmaster. A modern tradition dating from Joe Haines through Bernard Ingham and Alastair Campbell (with a game but forlorn attempt by John Major to buck the trend). The PM's Press Secretary, although nominally a member of the Civil Service, is in fact a key political figure whose professionalism and effectiveness is far more important than any cabinet minister to the conduct of government. The remarkable thing is that the Presidency achieves all that it does with the media on such a shoestring operation — there are not hundreds of "spin-doctors" and the outcomes that are achieved are a tribute to the grasp and effort of the small press team. For those of us who lived through the years when crucifying Labour was a daily media blood sport, we know we owe the Mandelson/Campbell operation a great deal. Nonetheless, I find it unremittingly depressing to have my low expectation of the level of media interest in politics confirmed by reading the exchanges between the Press Secretary and the media (available on the No 10 web site) at the twice daily briefings.

The strength of the media has helped to change the relationship between Prime Minister and party. It has almost completely turned around the traditional role of Prime Minister representing the party. Now more than ever *the party represents the Prime Minister* — the "one-way track" identified by Tony Lloyd MP when standing for the chairmanship of the Parliamentary

Labour Party in 2001. Members of all parties are exhorted to act as "ambassadors" for their leadership — the exact opposite of the constitutional theory of MPs as ambassadors for their constituents. Policy is made at the top and must be communicated rapidly to MPs in order to be disseminated to local party members, the electorate and local and regional media. A change of leadership line necessitates the whole army shuffling rapidly leftwards or rightwards to ensure a coherence of view and lack of division. General acceptance of the leadership's values is no longer enough in an age when the media pick over every detail to find a story of split or dispute. This "line" or official view is given by the Prime Minister whenever the party is in government.

Ironically the media complains about "clones" who spout the party line when it was they who helped to create them by the way they portray alternative points of view as division. Labour in particular was seared by decades of negative coverage by the Conservative oriented press. This need for parties to develop disciplined defensive strategies against the media has abetted the 'Presidentialisation' of politics far more than any alleged personal trait of "control freakery".

To the electorate more than ever before the current party leaders are the party. Tony Blair is the Labour Party and Iain Duncan Smith is the Conservative Party in a way in which Keir Hardie and Balfour never were. Laborious and often fractious debate and glacial policy movement no longer have a place in an era when Prime Ministers can be doorstepped and their reactions instantly relayed to every living room in the land. This is not a criticism. It is the way things are in an electronic media age.

I ask later whether Prime Ministers actually revel in this relationship with the media or whether a more serious counter-attack could be mounted against this exclusivity if they wish. What is not in doubt, despite a few snide references to Presidentialisation (starting with "President Wilson" in 1964), is that the needs of the media have promoted rather than hindered the development of the modern UK Presidency.

The End of Cabinet

I do not wish to go over the topic of the decline of British cabinet government, as has been done to death elsewhere. No one today other than the most self deluding cabinet minister or frustrated permanent secretary pretends that the cabinet is an important policy forum. However the state of the cabinet does tell us a great deal about the modern UK Presidency.

The increasing marginalisation of formal cabinet committees, the supervision of cabinet ministers by what the Deputy Prime Minister has called the "teenagers" from No 10's policy and political offices, the increased use of "Bi-laterals" with individual ministers, No 10 dealing directly with issues without the relevant minister being present (exemplified by the Ecclestone interview at No 10 on Formula One and tobacco advertising): all these acknowledge the end of cabinet. These trends have been evident for decades but have been taken further with each modern Prime Minister. They also suit the current Prime Minister's style. Working with Tony Blair in opposition I became used to the constant cancellation of team meetings and of the need to influence events informally; a style which has carried on in government. One cabinet minister told me "the PM just does not like large meetings". The epitaph to the cabinet was given by the No 10 aide who remarked to Professor Dennis Kavanagh:

> *Cabinet died years ago.* It hardly works anywhere else in the world today. It is now a matter of strong leadership at the centre and creating structures and having people to do it. I suppose we want to replace the Departmental Barons with a Bonapartist system.[3]

It is certainly true that the cabinet used to have an important institutional role in representing political pluralism within the governing party. In modern times, cabinets of both the Labour and Conservative parties have often reflected an internal balance within the political party, be it ideological or geographical. Harold Wilson balanced and juggled his cabinet with great care, as did Jim Callaghan — developing this to such a fine art that no regional, sectional, or party interest could ever claim that there was not someone in the cabinet who was relatively close to their view. This meant that *all sections of ministerial and back bench opinion felt they had some stake* and voice in collective decision making and were not merely supporters — safe pairs of hands fielding the pearls of wisdom which fell from above. The modern UK Presidency however has strengthened such that it has been able to break free of this informal check.

Once again Thatcher unwittingly took the presidency on further and broke the mould by clearly and often publicly defining the insiders and the outsiders in cabinet, inexorably purging the "one-nation" cabinet members with each reshuffle. No longer were there numerous examples of cabinet ministers who derived their power from the party interests, the ideological strain that they appeared to represent or experienced heavyweights who could run a major department of state without supervision. The trend has continued and is evident in recent cabinets. This is not to say that those who are in the cabinet should be denigrated as Blair clones. Rather it is true that virtually no cabinet minister can be said to be there as a representative of anything other than the Prime Minister's government:

> The Prime Minister is operating as chief executive of various subsidiary companies, and you are called to account for yourself. A good process [he added loyally].[4]

The sole exception to this could be John Prescott, whose post as Deputy Leader of the Labour Party (who would take over should the PM be incapable) is not in the gift of the Prime Minister but is one elected by the Labour Party as a whole. John Prescott is often portrayed as representing the Labour Party within the Labour government and while undoubtedly this is true he does so from the position of an elected officer of the Labour Party, not necessarily because he is the Prime Minister's choice for that role. Were Mr. Prescott not to be his deputy, the Prime Minister would be as free to move him as he has been with other cabinet ministers. But even his ambassadorial role on behalf of the party may disappear after the recent innovation of

---

[4]   Jack Straw, quoted by Peter Hennessy, *The Times*, 25 Sept 2000.

the Prime Minister appointing the Chairman of the party following the 2001 election. Because of this freedom from the constraints of sectional interest, recent UK Prime Ministers are freer to act presidentially and to make decisions without recourse to the advice and consent of cabinet members than ever in the past.

A further constraint which may not exist for the next Prime Minister is the personal relationship with the Chancellor. Contrary to widespread media invention, the close working friendship of Tony Blair and Gordon Brown has continued from opposition into government. In the first term there was a rough division of labour — to put it at its simplest, No 10 was happy to control the message while the Chancellor had more control over policy detail than his predecessors. The next Prime Minister will be unlikely to have such a close relationship with his Chancellor and hence could be even more dominant in Whitehall. Indeed there is strong evidence (not least due to the strengthening of the Cabinet Office early in the second term) that No 10 currently is keen to move from policing to policy, though the second term rule that Prime Ministers become more pre-occupied with international affairs may work against this. Some have argued that the very power of a Chancellor acts as an informal constraint on the Prime Minister. Peter Riddell, the distinguished commentator, calls this rule by a "duopoly", not a Presidency. However UK Presidents and prospective UK Presidents learn lessons and it would be of little surprise were the Chancellorship to rotate far more under future UK Presidents than recently. As Mrs Thatcher found, to leave this key post with one personality for too long (Howe & Lawson) can lead to dire consequences. Career development is non-existent in our essentially amateur politics in the UK and its absence at the highest levels can be catastrophic.

So, while the British cabinet continues to meet regularly each week it seems to do so as much as a status perk than an executive board meeting. *The Cabinet is a relic of pre-Presidential government* which satisfies a number of political needs — an audience, a chance to touch the cloth, a canvass on which to paint an acceptable gender and racial mix, a bit of networking outside the door

— but hardly ever now the opportunity to debate a key policy issue on the back of a weighty cabinet paper.[5] In the US this process was taken to its logical conclusion when in President Clinton's last year in office his cabinet went eight months without meeting him — only decorum prevents a similar thing happening in the UK today. In one sense it matters little to democrats how the UK President conducts his cabinet. It would be ridiculous to imagine that those who he selects for his cabinet would ever seek to hold him to account — a separate and equally legitimate institution must do that. Nor does there appear to be any desire from cabinet members themselves to change. From personal experience working with eight cabinet and shadow cabinet teams, I can say that personnel management, training, team building and esprit de corps rarely appeared on their radar screens. Hence there is not even a murmur that the Cabinet Office serves the Prime Minister not the cabinet and there is not even a pretence that the various new delivery, strategy, reform and performance units are anything but creatures of and for the UK Presidency. *"Collective responsibility" has joined "democratic centralism" on the scrap heap of defunct political axioms.*

For all the residual machinery that clutters Whitehall and Westminster — the comfort blankets from a past era — those interested in influencing politics must seek an entry not via the cabinet but via a member of the *UK Presidential staff.* As in the USA, studies of who are regarded as the most powerful people in the UK[6] show almost all the unelected, appointed set of key trustees around the UK Presidency are more powerful than any cabinet member — though none go through any ratification process by the legislature or are well known outside the Westminster village. It is here we find one of the more obvious superficial similarities with the US Presidency — with the Prime Minister having less and less reliance on the civil service machine and bringing in an ever larger team of unelected associates with him. These are people who do not pretend to reflect party, crown or

---

[5]   See Appendix 5.

[6]   For example *Observer*, 24, Oct 1999.

sect. They unashamedly represent and reflect (and often repli-
cate rather than complement) the President — comparisons with
Carter's "Georgia boys", Clinton's "Arkansas Mafia" and
Bush's "Republican Guard" are irresistible.

One area where the current Prime Minister took the Presidency in the UK further was that in May 1997 he walked into No
10 with *the first Presidential transition team in UK history*. They had
observed Thatcher for a decade, learnt, and were ready to rule.
They were a better prepared office than any of their recent predecessors, and these experienced staff, mostly from the office of
the leader of the opposition, were grafted onto No 10 on day one
of the government. This was a quantum leap for the UK Presidency.

The key Presidential staff are currently Jonathan Powell (the
Chief of Staff), Pat McFadden (Policy Director), Alastair Campbell (Communications) and whichever Lords are in the ascen-
dant — at the time of writing — Derry Irving, Gus Macdonald,
Charlie Falconer and Sally Morgan. The quality of these people
is uniformly high. The envy and mistrust that they generate is
due not to their quality but to their uncertain constitutional position and legitimacy. Lobbying the civil service and ministers in
the traditional way in order to ultimately get cabinet approval
may well be financially profitable for lobbyists but has little to
do with getting a political decision. While Prime Ministers have
operated with kitchen cabinets and groups of friends in the past,
the reality of the formalisation of the UK Presidency is revealed
at its starkest in the frozen smiles of those of us — including cabinet ministers, senior civil servants and the rest — who queue to
have a precious moment with the UK President's staff.

The Decline of Party

UK parties have been strong relative to other democracies, but
this has meant they have come into conflict with the growing UK
Presidency — only one of these institutions could dominate in a
unitary system that allows for only one winner. The Labour
party is the only major UK party to have originated not from a
split inside Parliament, but from an established external move-

ment which then sought representation in parliament. This led the party to feel that its views were at least as important as those inside parliament.

Unlike the Tories, *the Labour Party at least had a tradition of seeking to influence the government.* Often the instruments used to achieve this were crude in the extreme, for example, unamendable composite resolutions passed at the annual Labour Party Conference by block votes of trade unions after messy and bloody battles on the conference floor. The need to reform the party's policy forums and have sensible exchange was vital but it got caught up with the internal party warfare of the 80s. By 1994 the Labour Party had finally lost the taste for such warfare and had *submitted to its leadership* — the executive in waiting. A further election loss would have meant a 22-year absence from government, a burden too heavy for even the most institutionalised oppositionists to bear. There was briefly a window for a Third Way- restructuring and refining of the party and its institutions so as to provide for genuine consultation without rendering the putative executive operationally incapable. However the moment quickly passed and a new leadership in 1994 took full advantage of the craving of a party for power and rammed home the essential modernisation of the party which swept away with it any hope for an effective forum for the party to have a dialogue with its own leadership should it ever come to power. Recent years have seen ever more elaborate machinery to "consult" and "involve" Labour members and MPs but contentious subjects are avoided and barely a soul believes that anything other than the leader's view prevails. For example no organ of the Labour Party has discussed whether or not to join the euro — including the cabinet. Once again the party would find that the absence of an internal means of policy exploration would throw dissenters (that is anyone that had a view contrary to the leadership) into the arms of the only remaining forum that would give them exposure — the media, keen to present dissent as division.

The same process by which the Labour Party had failed to create new forums and so had surrendered influence to its potential

Labour government had already occurred in the only other forum for debate with the leadership — the Parliamentary Labour Party. It too had been seared by the debates of the 80's, the splits and divisions that had put the party within 2% of third place oblivion in the 1983 General Election.[7] Neil Kinnock had clawed the Party away from the electoral abyss but the necessary price was that "all good men must come to the aid of the Party" — a new conformity and discipline necessarily swallowed by Left, Right and Centre in the party. Even at a time of such pressure it remained incumbent upon the leadership, while blocking off illegitimate dissent (Militant Tendency etc.), to create *constructive channels for new ideas* and forward thinking. In the heat of battle the willpower to create such an irritant was not forthcoming.

The price paid is high — not having an effective party forum means not just a frustrated party which does not have a means of expression, it also denies the leadership a healthy competing source of advice to that proffered by a small coterie around the executive. This is to mistake alternative views for destructive criticism. In its turn this is as short sighted and damaging as the resolutionary politics which promoted it in the 80s.

In a unitary political system such as in the UK, the winner takes all. A UK Presidency has little need to compromise with other residual political institutions, indeed to do so implies weakness. There is no constitutional compunction to discuss or negotiate. Instead, to manage discontent and keep people happy, the rhetoric of "listening" is deployed — which is at best soft opinion polling and at worst a deception when decisions have already been made.

The desperation of political parties for office and their consequent need to *reduce visible disunity* has given the evolution of the UK Presidency one more ratchet. The Conservative Party structure was never likely or willing to stand in the way of the development of the UK Presidency. They always believed that their leadership should have a free rein. The old Labour Party was

---

[7] Tories 42.4%; Labour 27.6%; Lib/SDP alliance 25.4%.

always temperamentally and culturally likely to question the executive — New Labour explicitly was not. Labour now replicated (in this limited context only) the traditional stance of the Conservatives and removed one of the last feeble informal checks on the development of the UK Presidency.

Party members and structures are now being reshaped by the consequences of the Presidency. A growing awareness of the Presidency in the UK has highlighted the sense that one person or a key group can seize control of a party or have the party gifted to them in order to recapture electoral success. Both main UK parties provide examples of this; and of its opposite, choosing as leader your party favourite rather than the person most electable.

Of course the tolerance of the party for its use as a vehicle for the UK Presidency can be stretched too far and can place stress on the Presidency's control of the party. If a party with an acute sense of the need to capture power in order to fulfil its principles seeks to find as its leader the best chief executive available then, just as with managers of football teams, the price of failure can be exacted just as swiftly. The Labour Party however has little experience of this. In politics succession planning is an inexact and rarely practised art. Labour should be thinking about these possibilities now — though the machinery does not appear to exist for such thinking — because when the time comes we will not only be electing a new leader of the party but perhaps the British President as well.

The Ethic of the British Civil Service

Regardless of which Party has a majority in Parliament the British permanent senior civil service goes on — even in an era of change. The growth of the UK Presidency has had a powerful ally in the British civil service — it generally craves powerful and clear direction and abhors the confusion of pluralistic debate.

The civil service machine is traditionally suspected by politicians of all parties of having its own agenda. Yet it only really puts forth that agenda in the absence of clear political leadership. It could be argued that politicians in the past have been all too easy to seduce, allowing the machine to run in its own faultless way rather than seizing the agenda, redirecting the machine and being responsible for their own mistakes.

I well remember a conversation in the members tea room in the House of Commons with that worldly old Bassetlaw MP Joe Ashton. I was saying how much I enjoyed the TV comedy series "Yes Minister" where a smooth senior civil servant always manipulates his political master to do what he wants. "I never laughed at that" said Joe gloomily "It was too much like the last Labour government". In many ways the civil service took the edge off political and Presidential power, making it all less obvious and less unseemly. Now however the civil service does have an agenda. *It has the Prime Minster's agenda – more clearly than at any time in the past.* While civil servants regret the diminution of cabinet committees and management by informed advice, they equally know that even those ministers who want to run their parts of the machine can only do so if No 10 agrees.

It was again Mrs Thatcher who cranked up the Presidency and shredded another informal part of the unwritten constitution by becoming the first modern Prime Minister to reassert loudly and publicly the primacy of politics and to make it crystal clear that the civil service was there to serve. This should have been welcome — not just because of its honesty, but because it reasserted the fundamental principle that politics should be in control. The problem however is not one of politics being foremost but of unchecked and monopolistic political power being concentrated in the Presidency and served by the civil service. *Mrs Thatcher exposed the extent of UK Presidential power* in her public and aggressive use of it. Pretending that we do not have a UK Presidency would never be possible again. But nonetheless while it was she who made this relationship transparent — for those who care to see it — it was one that other Prime Ministers had or could have had if they had chosen to.

Despite everything said up to this point about the massive powers of the Prime Minster we should *not confuse powers with control.* It often seems that the Prime Ministers are seeking finger tip control, for example of service delivery. The British civil service and Prime Ministers seem to believe that given sufficient energy, and willpower they can always make things happen to order from the centre, despite the complexity of modern society. This leads to Prime Ministerial frustration when commands are not or cannot be carried out, which in turn leads to more task forces, in-house "units", personal reporting to the PM, more *overload* at No 10 instead of a rational division of labour putting responsibility at the lowest appropriate level. It also *mistakes decentralisation for devolution.* John Smith's concept of passing power back to the nations of the UK and putting it beyond effective recall is very different to devolving some administrative power which is on loan at the Prime Minister's pleasure. In many ways the same applies to letting the legislature do the job it is elected and fitted for, rather than seeing it as a problem to be managed.

The civil service has felt threatened by and never understood pluralism — debate is synonymous with gridlock, democracy is carrying out orders, localization and subsidiarity means a diminution of their control — so why should they push "the PM" in its direction? The quiet relegation of English regional government exemplifies this. The Prime Minister, never very keen on regional devolution in the first place, has been so "Yes, Prime Ministered" away from it that the first regional elections for England are still to be timetabled.

The result is a hide-bound inflexibility, still mistaking its 100 ways of saying no to local initiatives for decision making, still collaborating in rendering parliamentary scrutiny ritualistic and perfunctorily, cravenly throwing in its lot with the executive against all comers. Despite adopting all the new management speak and training courses, the ruling ethic from the top of the service still smacks of the UK being *the last country in the empire,* with native peoples in the localities, regions and nations of the UK still incapable of making their own decisions and their own mistakes. This world view is easy to sell to a UK Presidency which can be held publicly responsible for everything and has no institutional partners of equal weight to balance its judgment. All this makes for a stronger Presidency but poorer governance.

Personalisation of Politics

The weakening of ideology and the improvement of communications means that the style of modern politics has become much more personal, aiding the decline of cabinet government and the rise of the UK Presidency. On the one hand the historical ideology and tradition of a party is less relevant and inhibiting, and on the other hand the powers now inherent in the Presidential individual allow him or her to devise and execute a more *personal project* than at any time in history.

Some Prime Ministers take care to clothe this more than others in rhetoric that is comforting to their party. Mrs Thatcher had a strong Conservative conviction, though not necessarily one that was the dominant conviction of her party. Nonetheless her free-market theory was as identifiably Conservative as one nation Conservatism. However, the concentration of power in the leader, the Prime Minister, means that the party will forgive a degree of deviance just so long as the Prime Minster is seen as an electoral asset.

The current Prime Minister has taken this a stage further. He knows that in the modern Presidential era, distance from the party is actually an electoral asset. He is the first (but won't be the last) successful Labour leader to revel not in the party's history but in confronting and remaking the party:

> I believe we won a second term so decisively in part because we were a different sort of Labour Party. We are modern social democrats.[8]

The public find it easier to connect with one Presidential individual and feel less affinity for party bureaucracies and factions. It also taps into the popular sentiment that if you can run the Labour Party, running the country must be easy. Screams from party activists, particularly trades unionists, are a signal to the electorate that a Labour Prime Minister is his own man and must

---

[8]   Tony Blair quoted in *The Times*, 5 August 2001.

be doing a good job. If they stop screaming a few judicious Prime Ministerial shakes of the tree can soon start them up again.

However, with the increased freedom from party and its policies comes the responsibility for the UK Presidency to define the personal project and its policies. In the US the concept of using the Presidency as a "bully pulpit" to promote a view and a vision is well known. In the UK Callaghan's education crusade was an example of this followed by countless examples from Thatcher. Shorn of the John Smith democratic agenda we still await definitions of the Blair Presidency's big issues — centralised management and target setting for public services, vital as they are, do not have an historical ring to them. It may be that governing competently, decently and non-ideologically may be the legacy.

Most of the above factors have helped move British politics from *party-centric to leader-centric*. This dependency, some would say over-dependency, on the skill and performance of the leader of the party has led to a situation of great dominance of the individual leader. While this is evident in all Prime Ministers in the last 40 years it has reached its apogee in the last 10 years. The truth is that once the leader is established the party needs its President more than the President needs his party. This puts a modern UK President in a very strong position — parties have to tolerate far more from their leader. Mrs Thatcher heaped years of humiliation and contempt upon her colleagues before they finally snapped. Any modern party now has to think even more carefully than before about the consequences to itself of separating from its Siamese twin. Parties could themselves be mortally wounded in the separation process. The over-identification with Mrs Thatcher led to problems when the Conservative Party separated from her, which over a decade later they are still working through. Term limits or retirement ages are just two of the ways in which formalisation of such parting could be made less destructive, if parties and leaders could ever bring themselves to think of, and plan for, the day when they will not be together.

Whoever reaches the office of Prime Minister now inherits the UK Presidency whether he or she wants it or not. I have already mentioned John Major, who was ultimately forced to use the office even though he may have been more comfortable as a Baldwinesque collegiate Prime Minister. While the man is delineated by the office there is still immense room for personal style. In the USA Presidents have ranged between do-nothing Coolidge to hyper-active Kennedy. However in the USA if a President is less active, Congress has a tendency to fill the space. In the UK the Presidency is so dominant that unwillingness or inability to use the powers would create a vacuum with no obvious institution to fill it. And of course nature (i.e. the media!) abhors a vacuum.

Once established, the UK Presidency is supreme and can pull up the ladder from Parliament and party. It is likely that in future UK Presidents will have less and less time for the political class or indeed Parliament. Their closest advisors will tend not to be elected people but appointees and personal friends. Even ministers and arguably secretaries of state are of little real importance and can be swapped or dropped at will regardless of their ability.

This concept of centralised personalised politics is abetted by our unwritten constitution. *In a grotesque way we are seeing in the UK what might have happened in the USA had they not had a written constitution.*

A system which has projected a person to such supreme office might seem to them to be pretty unimpeachable. The temptation might be to feel that what has been good for them might provide a model for government elsewhere. It is a mistake to imagine that personalisation of power can be easily transplanted. While their own energy and historical accident mean that UK Presidents and their teams have an impressive and well-developed system in place at national level, that strong power base is rare elsewhere in UK politics. There has been an attempt to replicate aspects of Presidentialism in London, and eventually other cities, by super-imposing mayors — although in belated homage to the *separation of powers*, the London Mayor is balanced by a separately elected Assembly. As the recent difficulties of both parties in naming their candidates for London Mayor prove, not everyone has the assets, media access, and resources of the UK Presidency. Personalisation of power in the UK has been created by a unique set of evolutionary circumstances, not by the political abilities of whoever is the incumbent.

There is no doubt that politics has been personalised in the shape of the individual at the top of British politics and that this in itself has further aided the Presidentialisation of our politics. It is a trend that is likely to grow stronger even if effective countervailing limitations are instituted.

In conclusion, we have originated an executive system in the uk which has allowed the evolution of a form of government shaped by circumstances and events of this century which *fits more easily into the concept of a unique UK Presidential system than an old fashioned Prime Ministerial one*. If we face this development squarely and honestly we are in a far better position to ask whether it is what we want from the UK Presidency, do we need it and how can we get it to work more effectively for all our people.

Chapter 3

Making the UK Presidency Work

While many learned works[1] have been written about the end of cabinet government in the UK and a few have alluded to the development of a Presidency in the UK, those which have talked about a Presidency have done so in negative or at best, neutral terms.

I disagree. My view may be a more original one: *not only does the UK have a Presidency, but it is a welcome and necessary development for the UK in the modern world.* Hard though it may be for people in the UK to accept, a Presidency is a perfectly valid, acceptable, indeed commonplace way of conducting an executive.

The Functions of the Presidency

The UK needs its Presidency and its powers should *not* be diminished. It is no part of my vision for reform of the UK Presidency that it should be enfeebled in the foreign or domestic setting. A Presidency set in a pseudo-Athenian democracy or hamstrung by warring domestic institutions or paralysed by internal veto would be no good for us globally, nationally or individually.

We need a strong executive for several reasons, most importantly:

- The need for prompt and decisive executive action in the modern political world.

---

[1] Foremost among which is Michael Foley's *The Rise of The British Presidency*.

- The need for clear and authoritative communication to the public.

- The requirement for "joined-up" government or effective co-ordination of public sector activity.

- The opportunity Britain has to influence global developments.

Above all, those who care about or want to reform our politics need to recognise and deal with the reality of British politics rather than continue to live in a mythical situation. A part of that reality is that we will continue to need strong leadership in our public affairs whatever democratic settlement we have.

The need for prompt and decisive action was never more obvious than in a war situation. In the USA the need for swift action by the executive in war persistently causes problems where it meets the rights of the legislature. In the UK there have been no such inhibitions. Parliament, unlike Congress, has no rights to fight over — its role limited to providing a suitably sombre and historic backdrop for Presidential statements. While there may be an argument to formalise reporting to Parliament, that should not inhibit the ability of the executive to continue to decide and act speedily in these situations. War making, including anti-terrorist actions, is an executive prerogative — even cabinet involvement is problematic. It has been so in living memory, most recently in Mrs. Thatcher's conduct of the Falklands War and John Major's conduct of the Gulf War. The style of the current Prime Minister in preferring to work outside cabinet, allied to the needs of two wars in Iraq and the Balkans very early on in his premiership, gave another spur to presidentialisation of the UK — in effect a small group of specialists worked for a commander in chief. The quantum leap of global terrorism that took place on September 11 2001 and the consequent protracted war against terrorism will present new problems, but it is likely to accelerate rather than reverse this trend. Such a way of working is appealing to the executive and to all intents and purposes has crept into domestic policy making. However, *the answer to this is not to paralyse the executive's ability to act but to have equally nimble and responsive democratic accountability and checks.*

Quick response in the domestic area is often essential, and electors through the media have a right to expect government to inform them about events. Whatever our feelings about the communications monopoly of No 10 and the media, the Presidency undoubtedly has the ability to get a message to the public in a timely and digestible form. This smooth service stands in stark contrast to the culture of secrecy that pervades the traditional government machine, the esoteric language and belated proceedings of Parliament, the inability of electors to get straight answers from their public services and the dead hand of the UK's class barriers. All these other areas need to be reformed or to reform themselves: until they do the Presidency will continue to fill the information gap without challenge.

Government today is extremely complex and for it to work effectively there is a need for clear lines of management and responsibility, both for delivery and accountability. The executive has to give the clearest signals to all the competing parts of its operations about the aims and objectives of the government. We can argue about how effectively this role is being carried out at any given time, but co-ordinating or "joining-up" these efforts requires a clarity that only a strong lead from the executive can provide

The UK also needs its Presidency to be effective on the global political stage. Britain can contribute a great deal to creating a new world order based on justice and the rule of law. Our unique advantages include our use of the world language (English), standing at the axis of Europe and North America and our legacy of diplomatic skill. We are positioned to punch way above our weight in the counsels of the world and a UK President with the inclination and domestic support could take the lead on developing global standards. These could start with environmental accords, but go further, for example in building workable standards of international judicial architecture covering extradition procedures, global war crimes and terrorism courts, international democratic education and new rules on asylum and on economic migration. The agenda is mind-boggling, but presents great opportunities for a UK President.

In Europe, it could be argued that some UK Presidency or other could decide to leave its mark by immersing us in, or taking us out, of the European Union. This demonstrates not only the strength of the current Presidency but also the weakness of our other domestic political institutions and the urgent need to renovate them so that any such fundamental decisions are taken consensually. If the European project is to progress it must have consent and understanding, especially (but not exclusively) from the British people. The UK President could — particularly if legitimate himself — bring that sense and requirement to the conference table and help deal with the democratic deficit in European decision making.

If the UK is to play its part in global and European politics, these questions need a rallying point; a clear lead and expression of our ambition. Britain needs its Presidency.

For those who would continue to heckle the activity of the UK Presidency, what are the alternatives? We could of course continue the pretence that we do not have a Presidency, that Parliament rules and holds the executive to account, and that this blissful state is as close to perfection as politics can come. Many MPs already live on that planet. Equally we could seek to end executive domination by allowing another institution a turn at "winner takes all" politics — perhaps severely hamstringing No 10 and building a Parliament which is really in control and which oversees every operational decision. Or perhaps we could develop a federation where the executive's functions are residual and all serious decisions are taken by the nations and regions of the UK. Still another is to fold the British state and its President into some European entity. There are many other models, nearly all of which incidentally would need to recognise and confront the immense power of the UK Presidency in order to curtail and neuter it. They would also require the UK Presidency to be complicit in its own demise.

Recognising that we have and need a UK Presidency is only to recognise the reality of *political power*, we should not confuse this with *constitutional power*.

A different way is not to have a new winner of the unitary treasure trove but to *change the rules* (or create them for the first time)
so that a wide variety of political institutions have a legitimate
role to play, including a recognised and respected Presidency.
That is the pluralist alternative, of which more later.

Building the UK Presidency

There is a UK Presidency and it will continue to exist. In such circumstances it makes sense to recognise the political necessities
of Presidential power in the UK. Professor Anthony King calls
this the "reality principle". We may have different remedies and
futures but at least let us all start from the realities of today rather
than a pretence of where we are. Ironically, while it is essential
for an all powerful unitary UK Presidency to work efficiently,
that efficiency will become even more important should the
executive in the future be just one of several partners working
together — when expectations will rightly be higher. Executive
inadequacies which can currently be concealed will become
obvious when working with others.

In either eventuality there is a need to end the pretence that the
UK chief executive can or should run a major Western democracy out of a few rooms in No 10 and to confront the need to *build
a Prime Minister's department* on a par with a Presidential staff in
order to see through the responsibilities of the office. While the
UK Presidential transition team on day one of the current government was better prepared than any of its predecessors, sur-
prisingly few personnel were added in the first term.

The increase in staff at No 10 Downing Street during the
1997–2001 Government has been minute, (though requiring the
eviction of the Chief Whip from No 12 Downing Street and the
growth of the Cabinet Office) up from 130 to 152 at a cost of
nearly £2 million. Of these only 27 are "political" appointees —
though up from 6 under John Major. Nonetheless it indicates
that Downing Street is evolving a *Presidential department*, though
no one is allowed to admit it. A permanent secretary told me that
Sir Richard Wilson, the Cabinet Secretary, had asked his civil
servants at No 10 not even to mention the concept of a "Prime

Ministerial Department" to maintain constitutional fiction and not to frighten the parliamentary horses.

Maintaining this pretence helps no one. Formal recognition of the Prime Minister's Department could lead to the effective public and Parliamentary scrutiny of such a department. This strikes fear into No 10 when actually — providing it was done sensibly, not oppressively — it could be greatly helpful to it. The rise of the UK Presidency inevitably means the end of cabinet government and diminution of cabinet committees. It should of course not mean the absence of any corporate system for getting things done. Such a potentially powerful machine continues in the modern era to be run in an essentially amateur way. The modern UK Presidency requires neither the sclerotic bureaucracy of the traditional civil service nor the informal "who you know" confusion of a barrister's clerk's office. The end of cabinet government need not mean that everyone, from permanent secretaries to backbench MPs to lobbyists, needs a pal in No 10. Stories abound of poor follow up, relaxed process management, blurred lines of accountability — not all of which can be explained by personal style or inexperience of working corporately. The absence of systems for collecting inputs and information means an absence of decision making on merit which is compensated for by personal contacts and favours. Much of this could and should be put right by professional management and clearer accountability. The exercise of such supreme power would then be, and be seen to be, less arbitrary, more open and accountable, and more efficient.

Equally Parliament should not get anxious when weaknesses at No 10 are addressed by adequate staffing, resources and professionalism. It is in no one's interest to have an executive that is unprofessional any more than it is to have a legislature that is understaffed and undertrained. For example the restructuring in June 2001 of the offices in No 10 to cover communications, public liaison and political affairs — if it is a response to poor management and sporadic communication with ministers and MPs — is to be welcomed. Likewise the proliferation of units (see Appendix One) could help clarify the long-term role of the

UK Presidency if they have clear lines of account. Otherwise they will merely add to the confusion "I don't know how many units we have. Some of these changes are still being worked through" said a No 10 spokesman.[2] However, to help "deliver" policy objectives, these units should not be excluded in their terms of reference from examining the most constipating factor for delivery, the over concentration of power in our unitary political system. More special advisers too will help the Prime Minister's department execute strategic policy provided that they can resist the temptation to micro-manage and keep out of day to day delivery. Keeping the press function separate and tightly managed has meant that no special advisors from No 10 Downing Street have revealed market sensitive information in the local pub or written crass and insensitive emails, all of them and their masters become tainted after such indiscipline. It is important for these special advisors to work under a clear and strict disciplinary code as befits their privileged position.

In the US it is an accepted trait of the Presidency to have lots of advice coming in from different agencies, and equally accepted means have been developed by Congress and the judiciary to scrutinise this activity. In the UK we may have taken on this trait but do not yet have the balancing scrutiny because we have failed to acknowledge the truth about how the UK is really governed. The greatest service that the Prime Minister could do for good government will be to publicly accept that the office has so evolved over the last hundred years that now a form of Presidency exists in the UK, that its future should be open for debate and welcome that its performance should be constructively scrutinised for effectiveness, accountability, and value for money.

However, *to recognise and make more effective the power of the British Presidency should not be mistaken for an acceptance of unitary power*. While the UK President may be the chief of the executive and rightly sets the strategy, the execution of policy itself has to be devolved and localised to be effective. Even the flattest Prime

---

[2] *The Times*, 6 September 2001. See appendix 1 for an educated guess on who is responsible for what.

Ministerial learning curve ultimately concludes that even the most powerful office in the UK requires strong and effective political institutions working with it in order to deliver on the ground. To achieve their potential these institutions cannot be part of "command politics" directed, disciplined and exhorted from No 10. Such institutions — including Parliament, local government and public agencies — must be free to test and help forge policies rather than just carry out orders. They can be better agencies for front line delivery than Number 10. *Over-control means that the modern UK Presidency under-achieves*. It cannot do it all, but it could and must do a lot more in partnership with other political institutions. Being honest about the Presidency would help clarify and rationalise its functions and reduce the misplaced emphasis on Prime Ministerial willpower and energy as the major drivers of policy.

Many conservatives in all parties would be anxious that recognising the Presidency in the UK would undermine parliamentary sovereignty. However accepting the reality of the Presidency would in the same instant humanely put down the ailing myth of parliamentary sovereignty in the UK. The real question is not about maintaining a strong Parliament but *the inception of a strong Parliament* in order to balance and complement the powers of the Presidency. For democrats of all colours, accepting the concept of the UK Presidency would immediately redirect their thinking towards controlling the executive and rebuilding the legislature. it would prompt a massive change in how the legislature relates to the executive. Our problem is that our executive in the UK is the eighteen stone body builder and Parliament is one of several seven stone political weaklings. The answer surely is not to starve the executive but to nourish our other political institutions.

Hardly anyone apart from the most self-deceiving MP believes Parliament, as opposed to the executive, is sovereign in modern British politics. A once-in-a-lifetime fluke of parliamentary arithmetic does not negate that. In coming to terms with the UK Presidency, Parliament has an opportunity to carve out a clear role for its future. This is in the interests of all parties and their MPs. Socialism, Liberalism and Conservatism are not just part of our heritage, they can be vibrant and often relevant creeds which require a voice in a pluralist democracy in order to make a contribution. All of us in politics at every level need release from the cramping effects of over-centralisation. With political power escaping to European and global levels on the one hand and to the regions and nations of the UK on the other — there could be no better time for an honest reappraisal of what Parliament should be about and what an equal partnership with the executive might look like.

The other arm of the separation of powers — the judiciary — would also benefit from this unprecedented dose of honesty. Modern politicians have not expected a great deal from the judiciary and have rarely been disappointed — they managed for a period even to make that key principle of liberty, the rule of law, unfashionable. However in lieu of an effective Parliament they stood up finally to some of the excesses of Conservative ministers. Even with two landslide victories for Labour the opportunity for fundamental reform to mainstream the judiciary has been missed. It is deeply disappointing that of all the constitutional powers it still remains the most distant from and the least understanding of those it is meant to serve. For example, the exasperating way in which the legal establishment's interpretation has neutralized politicians' best efforts to tackle crime and anti-social behaviour on our housing estates has made the quality of life much worse for millions.

Even so the judiciary is capable of breaking out and heading back to the civil society that so needs it, not least since the Human Rights Act allows them even more constitutional elbow room. The question remains whether this elitist and still largely unreconstructed caste can seize the opportunity to be a real partner — always disagreeing when necessary — in a new democratic settlement. It should be remembered that the US Supreme Court, now regarded as an equal with President and Congress, developed its powers over time — notably establishing the right to judicial review of the Constitution in 1803. This demonstrates again that a formal settlement of powers is never the last word and that evolution can take place even in the role of the judiciary.

We can make the UK Presidency work more effectively and the renewal of the executive will lead us to question the role of the legislature and judiciary and be far more demanding of the level of performance which we are entitled to expect of all of them in a modern democracy.

Defining the UK Presidency

The Prime Minister's roles as the head of Her Majesty's Government, Her principal advisor and as Chairman of the Cabinet are not, however, defined in legislation. These roles, including the exercise of powers under the Royal Prerogative, have evolved over many years, drawing on convention and usage, and it is not possible precisely to define them. The Government has no plans to introduce legislation in this area.[3]

Nothing could better illustrate the lack of precision governing Prime Ministerial powers or underline the need for an honest definition of them.

Part of the problem of reform, particularly of something as central as the Prime Ministership, is the way in which efforts to reform it will be portrayed. The Prime Ministership is so pivotal in British politics that even constructive suggestions as to its future can be open to misinterpretation. The point is to examine the role of the Prime Ministership objectively and seriously and not have any analysis twisted into a personalised attack on whoever is the current Prime Minister.

Professor Peter Hennessy spoke to the All-Party Constitution Group (in June 1999) and outlined a view that the current Prime Ministership was Napoleonic. Tam Dalyell MP was so taken with this analysis that he spoke at the next morning's Parliamentary Labour Party meeting and accused Tony Blair of being Napoleonic. Needless to say, this was widely covered the next day in the press. Regardless of the merits of the Napoleonic analogy, Tam had made the fundamental mistake of seeing it as a Blair problem rather than a democratic and institutional prob-

---

[3] Prime Minister's answer to a Parliamentary Question from the author, 15 October 2001 PQ 1132.

lem. Serious analysis of executive power in the UK must constantly be wary not to fall into the same trap. This is particularly necessary today because the current Prime Minister's youth and media skills will any way give the appearance of a more Presidential style than his recent predecessors.

Contemporary political commentators tend to use the UK Presidential analogy about a British Prime Minister to suggest an over-powerful individual or an overblown ego, We must disentangle ourselves from this received wisdom. What problems there are, are *the product of the office not the incumbent*. It will become ever clearer that publicly defining and admitting that the UK has a system rather than a personality that is Presidential will have many benefits. I welcome the end of the illusion and I welcome the development of a strong Presidency in the UK. We need it — but just as importantly we also need it legitimised and consciously controlled, hedged about for our own safety.

We must decide what we want of the UK Presidency and what we want it to look like in 20 to 50 years' time. Accepting that we need the UK Presidency in the modern world would also help us redefine not just what the UK President should do, but just as importantly what it should not do. *The British Prime Minister is massively overburdened*. The Prime Minister has too many roles — party leader, Prime Minister, chief executive etc. A serious re-fit would be of enormous benefit. The truth is the UK Presidency has reached the limits of what it can achieve alone. The most cursory study of modern British Prime Ministers shows that executive power in the UK, even at its most extreme and unhindered, cannot do it all — even when led by its most obsessive and dynamic driver, Mrs Thatcher.

Even so there is incredible expectation placed upon the UK President because he is seen to be wholly responsible for all aspects of UK governance. This is the downside of monopoly power. In opposition, Labour MPs like myself deliberately drove Mrs Thatcher to distraction by asking her detailed parliamentary questions about the treatment of individual patients in hospitals of which she had never heard but for which she was "responsible".

Instead of the President being responsible for everything (and having to take responsibility for everything) it is possible to ensure that responsibility is taken at the appropriate level. Genuine devolution *relieves the centre of the need to seek fingertip control* of every aspect of a highly complicated society, just as a separation of powers allows the legislature and judiciary to carry out their legitimate functions without overbearing executive supervision. Congress in the US is regularly and rightly held responsible by the President where it fails to meet its responsibilities. This is far more serious than merely avoiding blame, it allows genuine focus on the areas most appropriate for executive action.

Redefining the UK Presidency would also be helpful to the revitalisation of political parties. The UK President should rightly be the most high-profile personality in any party. However, parties would need to re-assess whether he should actually control and run the party, not least if Parliament and local government had their own constitutional independence. Perhaps the role of party leader could fall to the majority/minority party leader in Parliament or better still be filled by a relatively unknown functionary — truly a servant of the party? Without this we are in danger of continuing the schizoid situation when one of the most important of a party's members needs to gain electoral credibility by demonstrating aggressive control of his own party. Like his US counterpart who does not pick candidates for mayor or governor, the UK Presidency could also then resist the temptation to get involved with every internal selection of candidates — for example the damaging disputes over who should be Labour candidate for the first London Mayor or First Minister of the Welsh Assembly.

A more pluralistic settlement always raises the question of how disputes and conflicts between different organisations are to be reconciled — an obvious role for a refocused Presidency. What machinery needs to be created which can handle legislature–v–executive disagreements, region–v–centre, or inter-regional debates? We need not be afraid of such difficulties and we can think through how to involve a plurality of institutions. The Presidency would have the key role in leading this process and being an effective partner in pluralism — the concordats already thrashed out with the recently created Welsh, Scottish and Northern Irish institutions show it can be done.

A UK Presidency with such a sharper perspective would, perhaps to its surprise, find support in the legislature. An active Parliament would relish its part in returning to the political mainstream and building the consensus necessary to pre-empt or smooth potential points of disagreement. How different a job from the current black and white oppositionist politics of Parliament today which flushes away so much of its talent.

Equally the UK executive could help to reorient our political system by making greater use of the European yardstick of *subsidiarity* — hopefully a little more than the European Union does — testing every power and function against the litmus of "what is the lowest structural level at which this authority can be used". For this to be useful and effective one institution would need to be able to access machinery to reconcile it with another and failing that make it enforceable ultimately in the courts.

For a nation used to a military hierarchy in decision making, re- assessing executive power and seeking to make it work better would be an uncomfortable leap into the future. Debate, disagreement, reconciliation were not the foundation stones of empire, they are the hallmarks of a future democracy and they are entirely consistent with a strong UK Presidency. We need our UK Presidency and it — to achieve its potential — needs our democratic instincts and structures. We all need to be honest about the present so that we can make the best of the future.

Chapter 4

The Future of the UK Presidency

The choice now for the UK is not between a Presidency or a Prime Ministership, but between an unregulated Presidency and a regulated one. My argument is not that a British Presidency should exist but that *it already exists,* and that it exists in a form that has never been legitimised or adequately checked and balanced and that we should now look to accomplish both of those tasks. There are a number of ways in which we could move forward on this. What follows is by no means prescriptive — indeed there is a massive scale of responses from incremental change through to a new constitution.

The US Presidency sprang all but fully-fledged from the constitutional settlement of 1788 that consciously sought to inhibit it. The UK Presidency institutionally is a giant surrounded by pygmies, not bound by anything more tangible than convention — the very nightmare that motivated the founding fathers in the US.

In the move from an unplanned evolved UK Presidency to a conscious one, the frame of reference we bring to bear on this question will lie in the context of Britain's development of a new democratic settlement. Some of the pieces for the settlement are already in place. The 1997–2001 Labour government moved smartly on implementing the John Smith agenda on the first step towards a Bill of Rights, the first stage of reform of the second chamber, Scottish Parliament and Welsh Assembly. However a further dose of inspiration is needed if the momentum is not to be lost. A new vision must be stated so that we can set realistic legislative targets. That vision can no longer exclude from serious review just one institution, the most important part of the political structure, our executive — the British Presidency. To proclaim that every institution in British society must come to terms with change, then *to pretend that our most important institution is either flawless* or beyond change is inconsistent, insulting and no longer acceptable. The charge of arrogance is always levelled at Prime Ministers, and is almost always inaccurate. However to dictate change management to every office but your own would make the charge justifiable. While the coming debate may find its focus initially around the need for better government, it will inevitably move on to the need for more legitimate government. Either way the ever-wider realisation that we have a mighty, unelected, Presidency will become ever more important in our politics until it becomes the dominant issue of our times. It will be resolved and reformed, the only question is when.

Outside observers are often amazed that there is so little discussion in the UK about our current and future democratic form in general, and specifically about the overbearing role of the executive. In other countries these things provide the nourishment for everyday political debates. In the US, the power of the Presidency is under permanent review, in the developing European Union the pace and extent of executive growth is constantly debated and sometimes jarringly checked by an Irish or Danish referendum or act of British recalcitrance. Yet in the UK the British Presidency is the truth that dare not speak its name. Instead the executive, the media, the legislature and political parties all acquiesce in reducing political discourse to the personal and the trivial on the one hand or the esoteric and irrelevant on the other. It is incumbent upon all of us, particularly those in politics or who aspire to political leadership, to raise these issues for debate and not be content with pre-packed, pre-digested, McPolitics.

The Presidency Changing Itself

If a breakthrough is to come in the near future rather than after years of unnecessary and damaging attrition, then *pre-emptive change will need to come from the Presidency itself.* Outside support and pressure will be essential but the reality of the concentration of power in Britain is such that only a self conscious UK Presidency could swiftly effect change. We tend to caricature strong leadership in the UK as one that brooks no argument or dissent and which continually accrues further power. It will of course take great leadership qualities to break free of that stereotype and engage in meaningful debate and persuasion of hearts and minds.

There are several reasons why a Prime Minister might seek to open debate about the UK Presidency rather than *remain in denial.* Above all, the UK Presidency as currently constituted does not work as well as it should — it can lead to under-achieving governance. Realizing the full potential of government and our people will require significant cultural change. Progress here might most obviously come about as an integral part of a new democratic settlement for the UK — a broad plan of the sort outlined by John Smith when Labour Party leader. John Smith's plan was driven by the confining effects of 18 years of Conservative rule. Today's drivers for a new democratic settlement would be the realisation, after one term in government, that if we are to achieve many of our goals they will depend not on ever more frenzied activity from No 10, but on *freeing up the political and economic talents* throughout all levels in our nation.

The second driver must be the great concern about declining political participation in the UK. Gone are the days when we could scoff at the low turn-outs in US Presidential races. We are now in the same league and urgent *reconnection with the electorate* is essential. To combat political cynicism demands that the political leadership of the UK examines its own role (above all its relationship with the media) and the relevance of the institutional losers in the unitary state — particularly Parliament, and local government. Their performance should now be of as much concern to the executive as its own performance. We must aim to restore faith in democracy by restoring the *fabric* of our democracy. While there are many areas where the UK Presidency could divest itself of responsibility — low participation and cynicism is one area where the executive must face up to its responsibility and soon.

What little media coverage there has been so far about UK Presidentialisation has tended to be over-personalised and superficial. There is room for serious discussion on this issue. In that context the UK Presidency may seek to *respond to growing public and parliamentary concern* about over-centralisation by *leading* public debate on the future balancing of division of political power in the UK. This could take place for pragmatic reasons, when the Presidency realises that over-centralisation brings with it isolation from and weakening of institutional allies who could help on service delivery, could shoulder some of the responsibility (and share the blame) and could improve value for money. Most attractive of all — it could be electorally popular to be the UK President who finally begins the national debate which enables people to understand and be more responsible for their own governance.

A key attribute that Presidential politics brings to British government, because of the massive powers vested in the premiership, is the unprecedented *ability to remake the British political landscape* — this could also help ease a way forward. In a previous era people complained that government moved too slowly or that when party control rotated, governments merely did and undid the work of their predecessors. Such was the power of self-policing and the web of conventions to inhibit government that it was quite tenable to argue that governments (especially Labour governments) were sucked into and rendered impotent by the ruling class. A modern British President however can seize the agenda and ensure our society moves as swiftly as an ever-changing world. Every British Prime Minister will henceforth leave an imprint of their "project" in a way undreamt of in previous decades. Indeed failure to have a project and move it forward will reflect badly on the incumbent, as with John Major (although in difficult circumstances). History may also judge harshly the first Labour Prime Minister for 18 years if he failed to use the two largest-ever Labour parliamentary landslides (majorities of 179 and 167) for a radical and irrevocable reshaping of our political landscape. Even those Prime Ministers who are not driven by a mission will need to use the rhetoric of change to convince us that they are giving a sense of direction to the enormous power of their office. Indeed the more conventional the agenda, the louder will be the spin about "radical action", "boldness" and "new revolutions". Unquestionably the UK Presidency has the power to reshape the constitutional setting in which it finds itself and one incumbent or another will seize that opportunity.

One question we need to answer in deciding how Prime Ministers might reform the UK Presidency is how conscious are Prime Ministers of the extent of their power. For example, did Mrs Thatcher and Tony Blair realise they were Presidents on coming into office or were they surprised they could do what they did with so little inhibition? Arguably Mrs Thatcher coming in from opposition could be in this latter category even though she did complain about the limits and constraints on her powers. I believe that Tony Blair — having studied and learnt from Mrs Thatcher's use of the office — is in the former category. As the debate develops all future Prime Ministers will be aware of the extent of their power. They may feel that while their powers could be overmighty, they nonetheless can personally be trusted with them. What is certain is that by the time Prime Ministers have been in office for several years they must be fully aware of the immense powers of the office. If so might a *Prime Minister have qualms about potential successors* using these powers?

Given the extent to which the UK Presidency continues to grow, with each new PM wittingly or unwittingly adding to its power or efficiency, the importance of succession politics grows. While using the power may be a larger priority than limiting it, it surely makes sense at the very least to set up an equivalent to a business "legacy system" team internally at No 10 to produce some scenarios for the future about where the office itself is going. In an era of low turnout, high political cynicism and weaker political parties, the prospect of unrestrained powers being exercised by someone who turns out to be an extremist party leader is an issue which must be addressed by every holder of the Prime Ministerial office. Our rights and liberties (even if we in the UK cannot always be told what they are) are not threatened yet by a rogue leader but why wait for the threat? This too could become a factor which encourages a Prime Minister to set down in writing or statute the *justifiable limits of the office* which he or she holds in trust.

As we identified earlier, part of the ability to reshape our politics stems from the increasing ability of a British Prime Minister to mimic what has been commonplace among American Presidents and that is to paint themselves as *outsiders* — acting almost as mediators between the electorate and government. They have come a long way since Harold Macmillan, the consummate insider who constantly pitted himself against the Treasury. Mrs. Thatcher revelled in shaking up "the government" — often as if it were nothing to do with her. Mrs Thatcher once said to a radio interviewer "That's terrible, the government must do something about it." I have mentioned that the current Prime Minister has taken this further, often appearing separate from the bureaucracy, from Parliament and his party. Oddly enough this distance is itself another factor that could make it easier for a UK President to reform "the government" on behalf of the electorate in line with broader democratic principles and not being beholden to any interest or institution.

The character of the *UK Presidency has changed* over time and it would be a nonsense to imagine it will not continue to change in future, but which way should it go? If the current or next Prime Minister does not define the UK Presidency it will continue to evolve according to circumstances and be defined by future holders of the office, perhaps at one extreme into a distorted rhetorical US model — a dumbed-down, media-feeding, sound-biting trivialisation of politics, personalised and oversimplified, assisting not just in the ending of ideology but in the ending of policy. Alternatively the developing UK Presidential machine might be used more ruthlessly. Imagine the use to which even a recent incumbent like Mrs Thatcher could put today's Presidential office of a beefed-up No 10 integrated with the stronger Cabinet Office. In these circumstances self-restraint or personal benevolence could be revealed as very flimsy constitutional bulwarks indeed.

There are then a whole raft of reasons why the Prime Minister himself might want to define his existing powers. He could be supported in this by other players. The *electorate* for instance may wish to be clear about the sense of direction on offer at an election. It can be argued that the UK electorate still votes on the basis of a perception of the manifesto that sets out a party programme and gives a direction which they expect the office of PM to carry out. A UK Presidency however will increasingly offer *mandate not manifesto* and is much more likely to want to develop its personal policy as it goes. The manifesto — already pretty vapid — could become meaningless and remove a further gossamer restraint on executive action. Those who care about our democracy may wish to have their view heard on this trend.

There are other political institutions in whose interest it is to define the UK Presidency — indeed the more powerful it gets the more urgent the need to act. We have mentioned the *need to arrest the decline of political parties*. The steady atrophy of local politics and local party activity has hollowed out structures of political parties to a dangerous degree. If they see this as a problem, then party leaders who aspire to the top office must address this urgently in the context of their own dominance of their party. Rebalancing the politics of the locality and the centre can only be aided by a reappraisal of the Presidency.

The over-concentration of power leads to dependence of the whole party on the UK Presidency. The President is the party in the public's view, so one slip, one resignation and all can be discredited. With no bets laid off in local, regional or parliamentary power bases, the whole party edifice is threatened if the Presidency makes a serious error. The political parties and their *parliamentary representatives* would feel comfortable with a debate

about the Presidency, but initially and ultimately progress on
this issue rests with the President personally.

The supreme test remains for the current Prime Minister —
can someone so adept, so comfortable with UK Presidential
power, step back and see what is so important if the new democracy he is helping to create is to grow after he has gone? For that
to happen he must use some of his remaining time to help to
*ensure that Presidential or executive power itself is defined, limited and
legitimised.* The list of modern leaders who have done this stops
with Gorbachev and De Klerk. What is certain is that if the Prime
Minister cannot do it, there is no one else in this cabinet or Parliament who can. Leadership now could pre-empt years of disillu-
sion with Presidential power and years of destructive attrition to
achieve what is after all, the modest ambition of making UK
executive power legal.

Legitimising the UK Presidency

The powers once exercised by an unelected Crown and con-
demned as arbitrary are now exercised (and some!) by the UK
Presidency. I have already stated that these powers should exist
and should be exercised by the UK Presidency, but if we in the
UK are to continue to call ourselves democratic they can no longer be so in any unplanned, unstructured and illegitimate way.
The first step to setting up the institution of the Prime Ministership for its fourth century of life is that *Prime Ministerial powers
must now be listed, openly debated and put in statute.*

Defining the accepted and acceptable powers of the UK Presidency in law will be a cathartic exercise and will need to be
thoughtfully managed. Sensible discussions are needed
between the executive and legislature to explore without com-
mitment what may be needed and how progress could be made.
We should not seek to prescribe the machinery for this but many
possibilities exist. Perhaps the Parliamentary Select Committee
on Public Administration might develop the trust of No 10
enough to begin work on agreeing a draft bill to describe for the
first time the role and functions of the Prime Ministership and
listing the myriad powers used under royal prerogative. I have

made my own small stab at this in my "Prime Ministership Bill 2001" (Appendix 4). Alternatively or in addition to this a conclave of past Prime Ministers could be convened under the auspices of a Speaker's Conference with a reassuring Downing Street secretariat. Equally the existing Cabinet Committee on Constitutional Affairs could prepare the ground. Any or all the above would be preferable to ever louder oppositionist sniping (invariably personalised and partisan) chipping away over the years at the acceptability of the Prime Ministership and deepening the open sore of cynicism about our democracy and its politics. There are lots of routes via which *a rational definition of Prime Ministerial power* can be arrived at and put into British law for the first time. One statesmanlike "big picture" speech — perhaps valedictory — from the current Prime Minister could be the catalyst and signal for this next piece of very British peaceful evolution. President Eisenhower's retirement speech, warning of the threat from the military–industrial complex, made many pause for thought about its significance and had a far-reaching and long lasting impact upon politics; our own Prime Minister is capable of nothing less.

In the short term one simple and symbolic step would be for the Prime Minister to put himself — immediately after a general election victory — before the House of Commons for formal ratification or election as Prime Minister. This process works currently in Germany where Chancellors such as Kohl or Schroeder are formally endorsed by the Bundestag without any detrimental impact on either institution's authority. Indeed it strengthens both. In such a reform it would be perfectly possible and acceptable to maintain the current ceremonial role of the monarch in the final anointing of Parliament's choice of Prime Minister.

In the longer term, being clear about which powers we all agree should be exercised by the executive will be a revelation. Attempting to list the current Prime Ministerial powers and those exercisable under royal prerogative is a Herculean task, apparently beyond even the resources of the Prime Ministership itself.[1] The mere act of listing all the powers and displaying their comprehensive nature will begin a further debate. Once that serious examination has begun, we will see that the most urgent and far reaching reform stems from the reality that the most powerful force in British politics — *Presidential power in the UK* — *has no direct electoral legitimacy*. The stronger the executive grows the more obvious will its illegitimacy become. The longer it goes on undefined the greater will be the feeling from public, press and political institutions that it is unaccountable and could become dictatorial. The UK Presidency needs to act ahead of the coming crisis of legitimacy. Restoring the rule of law to the highest office in the land will be a political landmark. At that point the discussion on a genuine separation of powers will start. It will be self-evident that one part of this separation is directly elected, the other part is not. We elect our legislature as a matter of course and would be appalled were we not allowed to do so or if , for example, the local MP was indirectly elected by and from local councillors. Why then should we not begin to seriously consider directly electing our President? *Many other western democracies directly elect their chief executive.* At the last G9 heads of government summit the leaders of the USA, Russia and France were all directly elected — nations not notably less stable than say Italy or Japan. Change has taken place continually in our political development, the end of monarchical rule, the introduction of election for parliament, the extension of the franchise, the abolition of the right of most hereditary peers to sit in the second chamber and devolving power to the nations and regions of the UK. Moving from indirectly electing to directly electing our President would slip neatly into this stately historical progression.

We have lots of *recent experience of far-reaching political change* and not just in devolving power to the nations of the UK. We also have recent experience in moving from appointed to elected Members of the European Parliament, then from one electoral system to another for MEPs. Once we get over the initial shock it

---

[1]   See the answer to my Parliamentary Question in Appendix 5.

soon becomes apparent there is no reason why we, the British electorate, are congenitally incapable of directly electing the most powerful office in the UK. Oddly enough the current Prime Minister has already passed legislation introducing a separation of powers and, although applied only to London governance, it is a welcome precedent. In addition local government has been instructed by statute initiated by the Prime Minister to split its unified structure into a local council legislature which supervises and holds to account the local council executive in the form of a Mayor or ruling Executive Board. Ministers in Parliament solemnly listed pages of reasons for imposing this structure on local government, blithely unaware that for every reference they made to putting right the inadequacies of local government they could have substituted the words "central government". There is no technical or procedural reason why we cannot move ahead — political will is the only prerequisite.

Of course the UK President is elected currently but only as party leader, not as President. The Labour Party's Presidential contender is elected by the Labour Party electoral college made up of votes from trades unions, constituency party members and Labour MPs. The Conservative's membership select their candidate from a short list of two provided by their parliamentary party. While parties might choose to retain these or similar systems to decide their Presidential candidate, we would be carrying out *the last great extension of the franchise* in giving all British electors a direct vote for the most important political office in our country.

Such an election could take place on a fixed term or at the same time as the general election, though Parliament may itself want to move to a fixed term when its life expectancy is no longer in the hands of the UK Presidency.

Once such debates had opened up *many questions on the nature of the executive and its relationship to the legislature would follow* — questions we need not be afraid to answer, questions other nations have dealt with, questions we do not need a nanny state to help us with. Should the contest be open to non-MPs? Should the President resign from Parliament once elected? Would we choose to run internal or external primaries? Would the President be limited to perhaps two or three terms or would it be open-ended like the Prime Ministership?

Once directly elected the UK President should be *free to select his or her own cabinet* (no longer limited to parliamentary colleagues) and to use the defined powers already agreed by Parliament. There are many precedents for Presidential style appointment in the UK. In the wartime years (1939–45) many non-parliamentary ministers were effectively appointed by Prime Minister. For example Sir John Anderson (a senior civil servant), and Ernie Bevin (trade union leader) were unopposed at by-elections in order that they could become MPs and then ministers. Prime Ministers subsequently often parachuted outsiders into safe parliamentary seats in order to get them into cabinet. Now that cabinet is less relevant it is easier to give the non-elected a peerage and take them into the inner councils, as recent Prime Ministers have done with little inhibition. One bonus from the UK President being able to do what he wants in drawing on a wider pool of talent, is that some of the ablest parliamentarians could be repatriated from cabinet acquiescence to take vigorous senior roles and careers as legislators. Indeed many might find themselves examining and confirming those appointed to executive roles by the Presidency.

As well as democratically endorsing our UK President, separate direct elections would give a new vitality to Parliament, especially the Commons ending its role as the house of government dependant upon the executive and creating a genuinely independent and distinct legislature for the first time in centuries.

The introduction of a separation of powers in the UK with the executive as well as the legislature directly elected for the first time would energise every facet of our governance and politics, legitimise existing realities and lay the groundwork for a plurality of political institutions to debate and agree upon our national and international direction. This development would release the most far-reaching democratic revitalisation ever seen in the UK. The executive could learn that it is OK to let go and not be controlling, not be responsible for absolutely everything — that other partners have to deliver. In its own way the US Presidency does this daily. Everyone in politics would need to agree new ways of working, interacting and consenting between equal partners. Executive, legislature and judiciary would develop ways of living and progressing together. The debates would never end — as a living democracy confronted and resolved problems as they arose.

A New Democratic Settlement

So, I am *not judging the Prime Ministership as right or wrong but as incomplete*, needing a statutory definition of existing presidential powers in the UK, followed by democratic legitimacy through the ballot box. All this would set in motion a wider constitutional settlement, including the regeneration of local and regional politics and redefining of the powers of the first and second chambers. As we have seen with the innovation of the Scottish Parliament and Welsh Assembly wherever one political institution is defined it inevitably begins to help define the powers and place of other institutions including the UK executive. Pluralism will begin to replace our current unitary system. The political biodiversity brought about by a separation of powers and devolution will begin to grow and strengthen our somewhat limited and in-bred political gene pool.

The main theme of this essay — the relationship between the executive and the legislature — may be approaching the end game. It is a story which has its origins in the English parliamentary revolution and battles of the 1640s, but that pioneer of democratic revolutions was partial and incomplete — a fact that has coloured our politics for nearly 400 years.

Now is the time to put that revolution to bed and be done with the Parliament/executive battles of a previous millennium. However for that to take place requires open public debate on what sort of political system we need, followed ultimately by legislative action initiated by the UK Presidency itself.

Directly electing the Prime Minister would of course take place after passing the appropriate piece of law. Passing that law would require great thought, perhaps new publicly accessible procedures, and be a novel experience for Parliament itself — a far more testing time even than the epic tranches of law required over 30 years on the last great democratic change in the UK — the integration into Europe and the devolution of power within the UK.

The reverberations of such a change would be felt in every corner of political life. People would begin to re-engage in civil and political society. Politics would again be exciting, everyone would have a reason to participate, Parliamentary and local elections could mean something again — a real attack on political cynicism could be mounted and local activity and public service could become respected once again rather than disparaged. The thirst for involvement and understanding of how we govern ourselves would lead inevitably towards requests for the whole UK democratic and constitutional settlement to be written out in plain English for all to see. The delineation of the key office would mean all the main institutions of politics had been defined in law, the Presidency being the last. All the parts of the jigsaw would be in place, putting them together would *reveal to the public for the first time their own British Constitution!* A terse clear exposition of who does what in the rest of our democracy is the right of all our democratic shareholders. Recognition of our political reality would then be extended beyond the Presidency, and include the other parts of our democracy — the legislature, judiciary, local and devolved government and the European Union.

Enough work has been done on the creation of written constitution for me not to get too involved in the detail of "How?" here. However a Royal, Parliamentary or Speaker's Commission could report to Parliament with a draft Bill to be examined and authorised by Parliament. My own favourite is for a UK Presidential Commission to be given this job — it would be the first ever such Commission as befits the importance of the task. A reinvigorated Parliament could easily design a programme to ensure that the first new constitution of the new millennium will be discussed far wider than by Parliament alone. Of course the provisions of a written constitution will be fiercely debated. That is to be expected and welcomed. The wider the debate the more understanding, involvement and acceptance there will be. Using TV and the Internet will mean we will have *a new constitution with millions of founding fathers*, not a mere handful.

Once the executive and both houses of Parliament had agreed a bill, such a settlement would need to be endorsed by a referendum. It would then need to be entrenched. Entrenchment — a novel democratic concept for the UK — would place legislative hurdles in the way of all who would casually seek to alter the democratic settlement without the same levels of understanding and consent that gave rise to it.

I do not incidentally envisage any change in the role of the monarchy. The largely ceremonial and symbolic functions of the head of state do not interfere with the democratic rights of the citizen and should be retained just as they are now. The monarch also performs an essential, if negative, task by denying to any politician the formal legitimacy of being head of state. Hopefully, whatever energies serious reformers have will continue to be directed at the hard target of executive power rather than the easy option of public pot-shots at the royal family.

A written constitution has also traditionally been used to define a separation from the past — the drafting of our own set of rules — a deliberate statement of new ownership, not least when separating from the British empire for example in the USA or the former commonwealth countries. It would have the same symbolism for the UK.

There is not a God-given split between societies which have and those which can never have a written constitution. While the US and French constitutions are revered as ancient (both 1791), the Australian (1900) and Canadian (1867) constitutions are relatively recent and the New Zealand 1986 Constitution Act is but a teenager. A constitution can be the product of open debate in a modern democratic society — it can be done without civilisation as we know it collapsing, indeed it would be a re-affirmation of confidence in ourselves and our civilisation. It could be used to underline the fact that the era of the management of decline in the UK had come to an end.

In the UK it will be even harder for us to take these first steps than Australia, Canada or New Zealand, not least since our hierarchical, class-based society is more programmed to give orders and act upon them. The political class in particular fear open debate as a "loss of control," it is a fear we must confront and overcome. The signs are good. Despite still being very close to the teething troubles of devolving power to the nations of the UK and initiating a Bill of Rights, we can see how quickly the situation is settling down. We have opened the Pandora's box of pluralism, thankfully we will never be able to go back.

The democratic reforms of the first Blair administration — the Prime Minister's homage to John Smith — have created a dynamic which in time will refresh and redefine the very executive which invoked them.

What Parliament Needs to Do

The processes described in the last few paragraphs are all predicated on the support of a proactive Parliament, one far more engaged than currently. The legislature's weakness in the face of the executive constitutes *the biggest democratic deficit in British politics*. At the moment Parliament's prime constitutional function is to provide democratic cover for the UK Presidency. An election takes place so that the leader of the largest political party in Parliament can assume the mantle of the executive and then, apart from occasional celebrity and keynote appearances, he can stay at a distance from the party and parliamentary midwives who bought him into the world. At this point a separation of powers does take place but it is grossly deformed with an all powerful executive on the one hand and a quaint, but largely residual legislature on the other. Thereafter no serious changes are allowed to the executive drafts of law which are ceremonially rubber stamped by Parliament before the Prime Minister dismisses Parliament for its 11 week absence in the summer. It is a measure of the development of the UK Presidency that not only the cabinet but the *House of Commons itself has now become part of the "dignified" rather than the "efficient" part of the unwritten UK constitution*, something unthinkable when Walter Bagehot coined the term during the high summer of parliamentary government, 150 years ago.

Parliament is the holding pen for those who are popularly elected — the most sophisticated political prison in the world. We can do much better. Parliamentarians themselves could begin to explore ideas for the democratic development of the UK. We must grow in awareness and confidence in the face of the executive. *If ending the "denial" of the UK Presidency about itself requires selflessness and vision from a Prime Minister, then we should expect at least as much from parliamentarians.* There is life beyond the constituency casework and the cheerleader role (important though they are), it involves building a legislature independent of the Presidency, with its own opportunities and limits. A directly elected UK Presidency would no longer need the cover of parliamentary approval. Parliament could then begin to find its feet as a proud independent institution with its own role in life.

What might that role be? It could begin to turn some of the parliamentary myths into reality — holding government to account, supplying redress, being the place for topical political debate. Of all these I would place at the top of the list the ability to *become the forum of the nation*. In the absence of an effective Parliament, political debate is necessarily played out in a distorted form in the studios of the *Today Programme* and *Newsnight*. There is no reason why a liberated self-confident Parliament could not recapture that daily agenda. Parliament would also end the Prime Minister's monopoly on initiating legislation; in future it would need to be mutually agreed with the executive and legislature — both able to promote bills. Parliament could revoke the leasing out of its chamber to the government and the shadow government for its stale and irrelevant slanging match (they could have nearby Westminster Hall) and instead use the chamber to hammer out a parliamentary view different from the executive view but — given the correct machinery and will — reconcilable to it.

We would also need to replace the ritualised, partisan, perfunctory questioning of the executive which passes for scrutiny and bring in media and modern management techniques, with extended questioning allied to more *mature and constructive dialogue with the UK Presidency and its cabinet*. Why close our minds to an MP or an Andrew Marr figure using the currently empty chamber each morning with a roving mike getting MPs' first-hand evidence live on TV on key constituency problems of the day, or a semi-circular chamber, or guest witnesses addressing the House, anything to get the House to speak to and for the electors and their concerns. Instead of leaden aquiescence every proposed bill could be subject to eight weeks intensive pre-legislative scrutiny involving outside experts and on-line interaction with parliamentarians and public, producing better and more widely understood law. The parliamentary committees which oversee departments would spring into life, though the burdens and responsibilities of disposing of real issues with consequences for electors (rather than producing reports in a vacuum) would be heavy indeed. The demands upon MPs would unsettle many who have carved out a quiet niche for themselves, but for most MP's — of all parties — it would be an opportunity to finally do some of the things which brought them into public service and politics in the first place.

A whole set of new working relationships with Parliament and the executive would be necessary so that business could be dealt with expeditiously. MPs raised in the British tradition would still rightly regard their primary job as helping the UK Presidency carry through the party's programme, but in future this would be a labour of mutual respect and involvement rather than dominance and rubber stamping. In July 2001 a brief flicker of parliamentary discontent led to the proposal that Departmental Select Committees should be elected by MPs themselves rather than appointed by the executive. Normal service was resumed as MPs were quieted by offers of committee places, but this small resistance against patronage showed that even in an era where executive power is getting stronger it is possible for Parliament to stand up and — win or lose — put forward a vision for itself which is not totally dependant upon the executive. *Imagine what Parliament and President could achieve together as independent legitimate partners working under the rule of law.* That imagination will light the way for the next serious change in British politics.

Conclusion

Within our lifetime the subcontracting of political action from the whole nation to one elite office will end and politics will be repatriated to our electorate and their representatives. An honest, open, *very British Presidency* elected by a ballot of all our people would rightly and fairly be a powerful institution. It would sit with equal status and recognition alongside a revitalised legislature, devolved Government to the nations, regions and localities of the UK and clearly defined human rights — set out for all to see in a written constitution. Radical as this agenda appears to us enfeebled creatures of centralism, it is commonplace in most western democracies.

The challenges which the UK Presidency faces are monumental. Relations with the EU, globalisation, climate change, terrorism, poverty and anti-social behaviour are but a few. They are challenges only a strong legitimate Presidency — deserving of our complete support and working in partnership with our other institutions — can meet. The time for pretence is over. Let us take the first steps from mythology to honesty in our democratic settlement by initiating this debate now. *Which ever British leader dares to state and accept the obvious about executive power in the UK could truly be the last Prime Minister.*

Further Reading

Walter Bagehot, *The English Constitution*, ed. Richard Crossman (London: Fontana, 1993)

David Beetham, Stuart Weir and Pauline Ngan (eds.), *Democracry Under Blair: A Democratic Audit of the United Kingdom* (London: Politico's Publishing, 2002).

Tony Benn & Andrew Hood, *Common Sense: A New Constitution for Britain* (London: Hutchinson, 1993)

Peter Catterall et al (eds.), *Reforming the Constitution* (London, Frank Cass, 2000)

Michael Foley, *The Rise of the British Presidency* (Manchester: Manchester University Press, 1993)

Jonathan Freedland, *Bring Home the Revolution: The Case for a British Republic* (London: Fourth Estate, 1999)

Peter Hennessy, *The Hidden Wiring: Unearthing the British Constitution* (London: Gollancz, 1996)

Anthony King, *Does the United Kingdom Still Have a Constitution?* (London: Sweet & Maxwell, 2001)

Peter Oborne, *Alastair Campbell: New Labour and the Rise of the Media Class* (London: Aurum Press, 1999)

Frank Prochaska, *Republic of Britain, 1760-2000* (London: Penguin, 2001)

Anthony Seldon (ed.), *The Blair Effect* (London: Little, Brown, 2001)

Anthony Seldon and Dennis Kavanagh, *The Powers Behind the British Prime Minister: The Hidden Influence* (London, Harper Collins, 2001)

Keith Sutherland (ed.), *The Rape of the Constitution?* (Exeter: Imprint Academic, 2000)

Appendix 1
The Presidential Office: Structure & Policy Advice

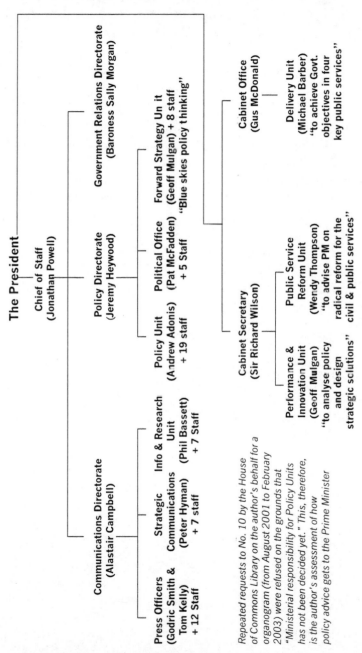

The President

Chief of Staff (Jonathan Powell)

Communications Directorate (Alastair Campbell)

Government Relations Directorate (Baroness Sally Morgan)

Policy Directorate (Jeremy Heywood)

Press Officers (Godric Smith & Tom Kelly) + 12 Staff

Strategic Communications (Peter Hyman) + 7 staff

Info & Research Unit (Phil Bassett) + 7 Staff

Policy Unit (Andrew Adonis) + 19 staff

Political Office (Pat McFadden) + 5 Staff

Forward Strategy Un it (Geoff Mulgan) + 8 staff "Blue skies policy thinking"

Cabinet Office (Gus McDonald)

Delivery Unit (Michael Barber) "to achieve Govt. objectives in four key public services"

Cabinet Secretary (Sir Richard Wilson)

Public Service Reform Unit (Wendy Thompson) "to advise PM on radical reform for the civil & public services"

Performance & Innovation Unit (Geoff Mulgan) "to analyse policy and design strategic solutions"

Repeated requests to No. 10 by the House of Commons Library on the author's behalf for a organogram (from August 2001 to February 2003) were refused on the grounds that "Ministerial responsibility for Policy Units has not been decided yet." This, therefore, is the author's assessment of how policy advice gets to the Prime Minister

Appendix 2
The Presidential Personnel
Prime Ministers Office
10 Downing Street, London SW1A 2AA
Telephone 020 7270 3000
www.number-10.gov.uk

Prime Minister:	Rt Hon Tony Blair MP
Chief of Staff:	Jonathan Powell
Director of Communications and Strategy:	Alastair Campbell
Director of Government Relations:	Baroness Sally Morgan
Principle Private Secretary and Head of Policy Directorate:	Jeremy Heywood
Advisor on EU Affairs and Head of the European Secretariat:	Sir Stephen Wall
Advisor on Foreign Policy and Head of the Overseas and Defence Secretariat:	Sir David Manning
Parliamentary Private Secretary:	David Hanson MP
Policy Directorate:	Andrew Adonis (Head of Policy)
	Simon Virley
	Geoffrey Norris
	Patrick Diamond
	Mike Emmerich
	Carey Oppenheim
	Derek Scott
	Ed Richards
	Sarah Hunter
	Simon Stevens
	Justin Russel
	Martin Hurst
	Claire Sumner
	Alasdair McGowan
	Matthew Elson
Foreign Policy:	Matthew Rycroft
	Anna Wechberg

Liz Lloyd
Roger Liddle
Francis Campbell

Head of the Delivery Unit:	Michael Barber
Head of the Office of Public Service Reform:	Wendy Thomson
Head of the Forward Strategy Unit:	Geoff Mulgan
Secretary for Appointments:	William Chapman
Executive Secretary:	Jay Jayasundara

Political Office

Political Secretary:	Pat McFadden
Assistant Political Secretaries:	Nita Clarke
	Sally Dobson
	Razi Rahman
MEP Liason/ Europe:	Rachel Cowburn
Director of Events and Visits:	Fiona Millar
Personal Assistant to the PM(Diary):	Katie Kay
Parliamentary Clerk:	Nicholas Howard

Communications and Strategy

Prime Ministers Official Spokesmen (PMOS):	Godric Smith
	Tom Kelly
Chief Press Officer:	Anne Shevas
Press Officers:	Martin Sheehan
	Tanya Joseph
	Helen Mason
	Ben Wilson
	Hilary Coffman
	Daniel Pruce
	John Shield
Strategic Communications Unit:	Peter Hyman
Research and Information:	Phil Bassett
Corporate Communications:	James Humphreys

Appendix 3
Comparison of UK and US Presidencies

<u>*UK Presidency*</u>

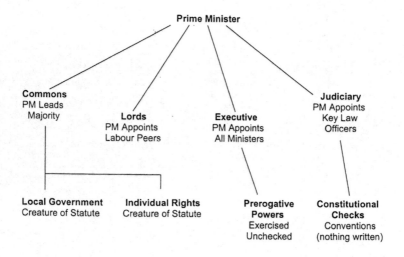

<u>*US Constitution*</u>

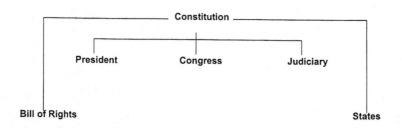

Appendix Four
The Prime Ministership Bill

On 28 November 2001 the author presented the text of the above Bill to Parliament and made a ten minute speech to introduce the Bill. Both the final text of the Bill and the speech are available from the author at the House of Commons or from his web-site www.grahamallen.labour.co.uk. If you would like to participate in developing this bill further please e-mail your comments to allengw@parliament.uk

The Prime Ministership Bill 2001 [1]

A Bill to establish in statute the office of Prime Minister and to define and regulate its powers, and for connected purposes

Whereas those functions and responsibilities and powers of the office of Prime Minister have never been defined in statute;

And whereas those functions and responsibilities and powers have vastly expanded since the office was first established;

And whereas in the absence of such definition the democratic accountability of the Prime Minister to the House of Commons, and to the people of the United Kingdom, requires clarification;

And whereas it is expedient to distinguish in statute the executive functions of government from the legislative functions of Parliament;

And whereas the use by the Prime Minister of Royal Prerogative powers is based on convention and has no basis in statute law;

Be it enacted by the Queen's most Excellent Majesty, by and with the advice and consent of the Lords Spiritual and Temporal, and Commons, in this present Parliament assembled, and by the authority of the same, as follows:

Appointment of Prime Minister

1   1)   The Prime Minister shall be appointed by Her Majesty and shall be subject to the consent of the House of Commons within 7 days of a general election, or the death or resignation of a serving Prime Minister.

      2)   Except in the case of a vacancy caused by the death or resignation of a serving Prime Minister, Her Majesty shall

---

[1]   Notes in italics are explanatory and do not form part of the Bill

appoint as Prime Minister only a person who has been declared to be a candidate for that office at a General Election.[2]

Term of office of Prime Minister

2   The Prime Minister shall hold office during the term of the House of Commons which has consented to his appointment. He shall resign if the House of Commons resolves that he no longer enjoys its confidence.

Functions of the Prime Minister

3   Except in respect of matters which are the exclusive responsibility of the European Union or any devolved Parliament or Executive within the United Kingdom the Prime Minister shall have the following functions:

   a)   to determine the policies of the United Kingdom government;

   b)   to communicate the policies of the United Kingdom government;

   c)   to execute the policies of the United Kingdom government;

   d)   to decide which measures represent the legislative programme of the United Kingdom government;

   e)   to decide on the level and application of taxation within the United Kingdom and the objects of public spending;

   f)   to recommend appointments to honours, other than those in the gift of Her Majesty or life peerages given to persons other than members of the Prime Minister's political party;

   g)   to appoint the ministers of the United Kingdom government and determine their responsibilities provided that

---

[2]   *This would mean that the Prime Minister need* not *be a member of either House of Parliament. The criterion is that he or she should have been declared as a candidate for the office of Prime Minister at a General Election. The Bill leaves it open whether this should be achieved by a separate election for Prime Minister or whether it could be left to each party to declare formally its candidate for Prime Minister should it win a Parliamentary majority. In practice, clause 1 would probably lead the governing party to name a Deputy to take over if the Prime Minister should die or resign.*

for each Department of State he shall appoint as a minister at least one member of each House of Parliament;[3]

h) to decide whether to declare war or commit United Kingdom armed forces to armed conflict and, if they are so committed, to determine their strategy and objectives;

i) to decide whether to declare a state of emergency;

j) to appoint the permanent heads of government departments, the members of the Defence Staff, and the heads of the security services.

Power to delegate

4 The Prime Minister may delegate any of the functions referred to in section 3 of this act with the exception of those referred to in sub-sections (g) to (j) inclusive provided that any such delegation is communicated to the House of Commons at the time it is made. Any action performed or statement made by a person under powers delegated under this Act shall be treated as if it were performed or made by the Prime Minister or by ministers acting under his authority.[4]

Power of appointment

5 To assist him in the performance of any of the functions referred to in section 3 of this Act the Prime Minister may

a) appoint a Prime Minister's Department without limit as to its size or membership, which shall be paid for out of money provided by Parliament;

b) appoint any non-departmental public body without limit as to its size or membership, which shall be paid for out of money paid for by Parliament;

---

[3] *There is no obligation for the Prime Minister to choose ministers from either House of Parliament, or to make them become members of either House after their appointment. However for each Department of State he must choose a minister from each House of Parliament. All ministers are given a general duty to account to Parliament under clause 9.*

[4] *Note: this recognizes in statute that the biggest decisions in government are reserved exclusively to the Prime Minister. It also means that he or she, or ministers, answer for anything done or said in his name. The line of accountability goes ultimately to the Prime Minister, but the clause leaves open two possibilities. First, a minister misused his or her delegated powers in carrying out the general policy assigned to him or her by the Prime Minister. In that case the line of accountability stops at the minister. Second, the Prime Minister's policy itself was manifestly unlawful or unreasonable – in which case he or she must answer for its consequences.*

c)   appoint any person whomsoever to the public service, who shall be paid for out of money provided by Parliament,[5]

Use of Crown Prerogative Powers

6 1)   In the discharge any of the functions referred to in section 3 of this Act the Prime Minister may advise Her Majesty to use any power or issue any command within the prerogative of the Crown other than that of dissolving or proroguing Parliament.

2)   Without prejudice to the generality of sub-section (1), the Prime Minister in the discharge of any of the functions referred to in section 3 of this Act, shall with the consent of Her Majesty have responsibility for any execution of the powers under the Royal Prerogative which are listed in Schedule 1.

3)   No immunity attached to the Crown shall be attached to the Prime Minister in the use of any power under this section.

4)   Any use of any power under this section shall be reported to the House of Commons, within seven days subject to any restrictions which the Speaker may agree as necessary to protect national security, or in the administration of justice or the prevention and detection of serious crime.[6]

---

[5]   *This gives a general power for the Prime Minister to appoint a Department of his own, or to make appointments elsewhere in the civil service or to public bodies.*

[6]   *This is intended to invest the Prime Minister with almost all the surviving powers of the Crown – provided that he uses them lawfully (he is denied the legal immunity of the Crown). Under clause 8 he would also be obliged to obey any resolution by the House of Commons. Subsection 2 and Schedule 1 are intended to allow him to use – and accept responsibility - for certain powers under delegated authority from the Queen, namely those most related to government. However, it ends his power to ask for a dissolution – because this whole section is linked to the PM's functions as head of government. So long as he can function, there is no reason why the Queen should give him a new Parliament. Only if the Queen cannot find anyone whom Parliament will accept as Prime Minister should there be a dissolution. The Prime Minister is not invested with any immunity given to the Crown. He is given the obligation of reporting his use of Prerogative powers to the House of Commons unless he can demonstrate to the Speaker that such reporting would have prejudice national security or the administration of justice or the prevention of serious crime.*

Powers of Secretaries of State

7 For the avoidance of doubt, any power under statute which may be exercised by a Secretary of State may be exercised by the Prime Minister. Any such exercise by the Prime Minister shall automatically cancel any previous exercise of the same power. [7]

Duty to behave lawfully

8 Nothing in this Act shall empower the Prime Minister, or any person acting under his authority, to disregard any provision of the Human Rights Act 1998, or any obligation under international law or treaty, under common law or equity or any other obligation to behave justly, fairly, reasonably and lawfully, or any published rules for the time being in force for ministers and civil servants in the conduct of public life, or to act in contempt of any resolution of the House of Commons.[8]

Duty to account to Parliament

9 The Prime Minister, ministers of the Crown and other persons acting under his authority, shall be under a duty to account to either House of Parliament in such ways as it may prescribe.

Public policy

10 For the avoidance of doubt, in any matter which is not the exclusive responsibility of the European Union or a devolved Parliament or Executive within the United Kingdom a statement by or on behalf of the Prime Minister shall be regarded as a definitive statement of the public policy of the United Kingdom.[9]

---

[7] *This makes it clear that the Prime Minister is a Secretary of State and therefore has supreme executive authority in any area of government. He would be subject to the same limits as any Secretary of State (ie he would have to act reasonably and intra vires) – for which see also the general obligation in clause 8.*

[8] *This clause may be otiose and is certainly meant to be declaratory. It aims to put on the face of the Bill a general obligation that Prime Ministerial powers be used lawfully and fairly. The final phrase aims to re-assert the ultimate sovereignty of the House of Commons.*

[9] *This makes the Prime Minister the supreme source of what represents public policy in the United Kingdom. His statements would be binding on public administrators, and on the courts (if they were deciding, for example, whether a contract should be void for public policy)*

Short title

9 This Act may be cited as the Prime Ministership Act 2001.

Schedule 1

Royal Prerogative powers which shall henceforth be exerciseable on the authority of the Prime Minister in pursuance of section 6(2) of this Act

1. To make Orders In Council
2. To declare war or commit United Kingdom forces to armed conflict.
3. To issue lawful commands to the armed forces.
4. To require persons to perform military service or to other service to the state in times of armed conflict or emergency.
5. To sign or ratify treaties.
6. To recognize foreign governments.
7. To appoint ambassadors, permanent secretaries of departments, the heads of the security services, members of the Defence Staff, Royal Commissions and members of public bodies.
8. To declare a state of emergency.
9. To order the confiscation, forfeiture or seizure of property and assets.
10. To issue pardons and detain felons or the insane during pleasure.
11. To institute or quash legal proceedings.
12. To assert Crown immunity in any legal proceedings and to grant public interest immunity certificates.
13. Powers in relation to intestacy, the failure of charitable trusts, treasure trove, mineral rights, wreck, sturgeon, swans, whales, territorial waters and the ownership of the foreshore of the United Kingdom.[10]

General Note: The list of powers deliberately omitted honours and peerages (mentioned elsewhere) and appointment of judges. The bill also denies the Prime Minister the prerogative power to commission army officers, police, tax commissioners etc – these people should hold their powers from the neutral Crown not a party politician. This issue will be considered again in the forthcoming Crown Powers and Privileges Bill.

---

[10] *This strange menagerie is intended to help Parliament focus on the arcane survivals of Prime Ministerial power or Royal privilege.*

Appendix Five
Parliamentary Questions

Cabinet Ministers told me that Cabinet discussions were no longer taken on the back of weighty civil service papers previously circulated in Whitehall; a viewpoint supported by Professor Peter Hennessy. To confirm the accuracy of this I submitted a written Parliamentary Question for answer on 15 October 2001 it read "When did the Cabinet last discuss a paper on policy which had been circulated for comment before the meeting". The question was returned to me marked "Blocked" with the further explanation that "Details of the proceedings of the Cabinet are exempt from disclosure for 30 years under the code of practise on access to Government information".

Even when questions from members of the legislature about the executive are answered they are not always too informative.

Parliamentary Question to the Prime Minister
15 October 2001   PQ 1124

Graham Allen: To ask the Prime Minister, if he will estimate how much time he spent on dealing with issues of presentation of government policy in the media in the last 12 months.

Prime Minister: "Issues of presentation are a matter for the Director of Strategy and Communication and the Prime Minister's Official Spokesman. I discuss these issues with them as required."

SOCIETAS: essays in political and cultural criticism

Public debate has been impoverished by two competing trends. On the one hand the trivialization of the media means that in-depth commentary has given way to the soundbite. On the other hand the explosion of knowledge has increased specialization, and academic discourse is no longer comprehensible. As a result writing on politics and culture is either superficial or baffling.

This was not always so — especially for politics. The high point of the English political pamphlet was the seventeenth century, when a number of small printer-publishers responded to the political ferment of the age with an outpouring of widely-accessible pamphlets and tracts. Indeed Imprint Academic publishes facsimile C17th. reprints under the banner 'The Rota'.

In recent years the tradition of the political pamphlet has declined—with most publishers rejecting anything under 100,000 words. The result is that many a good idea ends up drowning in a sea of verbosity. However the digital press makes it possible to re-create a more exciting age of publishing. *Societas* authors are all experts in their own field, but the essays are for a general audience. Each book can be read in an evening. The books are available retail at the price of £8.95/$17.90 each, or on bi-monthly subscription for only £5/$10. Details: **imprint-academic.com/societas**

IMPRINT ACADEMIC, PO Box 200, Exeter, EX5 5YX, UK
Tel: (0)1392 841600 Fax: (0)1392 841478 sandra@imprint.co.uk
imprint-academic.com/societas